Y0-BXR-548

NAPOLEON AND ALEXANDER I: A STUDY IN FRANCO-RUSSIAN RELATIONS, 1807-1812

Alexander C. Niven

University Press
of America™

Library of Congress Catalog Card Number: 78-60628

TABLE OF CONTENT

i

INTRODUCTION

This monograph is a study and analysis of Napoleon's relations
with Russia from the day of his alliance with Czar Alexander I until the
time when the cooperation between the two Emperors ceased and Napoleon felt
obliged to enforce his will once again by war.

A systematic study of Napoleon's relations with Alexander I has, to
my knowledge, not yet been made in English.

One of the objectives of this monograph is to trace the developments
in the various European countries which either contributed to an agreement or
to a disagreement between the two Emperors. Where necessary, a brief background
history is provided to facilitate a better comprehension of events and developments
between 1807 and 1812. The principal stress, however, is placed on Napoleon's
intentions in as well as for the various countries under his control. In this
manner one should be able to evaluate the extent to which his plans clashed with
those of the Russian Czar.

Napoleon's ultimate aim, one he pursued with all means at his disposal,
was the assurance of a permanent peace with England and a peaceful Europe under
French domination. The Alliance of Tilsit could have achieved both if only it could
have been consolidated according to its provisions and aims. The existence, however,
of several unresolved issues, such as the question of Poland, or, the difficulties
concerning the enforcement of the Continental Blockade, proved to be of such
importance to both Emperors, whose plans differed, that within five years of the
alliance, war became inevitable.

An in-depth study of these and similar problems which impeded any or all
permament agreements between France and Russia is this monograph's primary objective.

An initial study of "Napoleon's Russian Policy, 1807-1812" was originally
suggested by Prof.Dietrich Gerhard of Washington University. This suggestion resulted
in a Master's thesis at the mentioned university in 1954. The present work is an
extension and altered version of this thesis.

St.Louis, Missouri, 1978   Alexander C. Niven

THE TREATIES OF PEACE AND ALLIANCE
OF TILSIT[1]

The treaties concluded between France and Russia at Tilsit are divided
into three parts: the first consists of the Peace Treaty, intended for immediate
publication; the second consists of separate and secret articles; the third is
the Treaty of Alliance. All articles are closely related, and, together, they
provide the direction of future policies of France and Russia. The effect of these
treaties was a complete change in Russia's foreign policy. To make this better
understandable, an analysis of the treaties is necessary.

The first three articles of the Treaty of Peace deal with the cessation
of hostilities. Article IV shows in great detail the territories to be returned
to Prussia after the evacuation of French troops. According to Article V, the
territories which were Polish up to January 1772, but which were now owned by
Prussia, became the Duchy of Warsaw; the city of Danzig and adjoining territories
became independent (Article VI). Under the stipulations of Article XV, Russia
recognized the Confederation of the Rhine and promised further to recognize any
additional adhesions to this Confederation. An Articles XXI and XXII Russia
undertook to cease hostilities with Turkey and to evacuate her forces from the
Principalities of Walachia and Moldavia. Both Russia and France recognized their
respective possessions as they were at the time of the signing of the treaty;
they pledged themselves to resume commercial relations and assign ambassadors
to each other's government (Articles XXV, XXVI, XXVII).

The secret articles were of great significance for France inasmuch as
Russia abandoned to France the region of Cattaro (Kotor) and the Seven Ionian
Islands, including Corfu (Articles I, II).

The most important articles are contained in the Treaty of Alliance.
According to Article I, each contracting party promised to come to the aid of
the other in any war with any European power which might involve either of the
contracting parties. Articles II and III describe the joint military measures
and a promise by both parties not to sign a separate peace. Article IV concerns
England; it stipulates that if England should refuse to make peace with France
by November 1, 1807, Russia would join France in her war against this country.
Should this become necessary, the two allied powers would jointly ask Denmark,
Sweden and Portugal to close their ports to British shipping and to break off
diplomatic relations with England and declare war. Any nation refusing to do so

would be regarded as an enemy (Article V). Austria was to be approached by both powers to bring her into the war against England (Article VI). If England consents to the conditions of peace "to respect the flags of all nations upon the seas and restore all conquests she made against France and her allies since 1805," Hanover would be ceded to her in compensation for the return of French, Dutch, and Spanish colonies (Article VII). Lastly, Article VIII stipulates that if Turkey refused to accept the conditions of peace with Russia, "the two contracting parties will come to a mutual understanding for the purpose of liberating all the provinces of the Ottoman Empire in Europe, not including the city of Constantinople and the province of Rumelia, from the yoke and the vexations of the Turks." This Treaty of Alliance was to remain secret also.

The treaties were signed on July 7 and ratified on July 9, 1807. For France they were signed by M. Talleyrand, Napoleon's foreign minister; for Russia by Prince Alexander Kurakin and Prince Lobanof of Rostof.

A separate Peace Treaty was signed between France and Prussia on July 9, 1807.[2] Under this Treaty the articles concerning Prussia from the Franco-Russian Treaty are confirmed, but are described in greater detail. An Articles VII and X, for example, all cessions are given which Prussia had to agree to in favor of Saxony, as well as the territories between the Rhine and the Elbe which had to be ceded. Articles XVIII and XIX deal with the territories ceded to Russia, such as, for example, Byalystok and the city of Danzig. Under Article XXVII Prussia undertakes to close all her ports to English shipping. This Treaty with Prussia was signed by M.Talleyrand and by Marshall Kalkreuth and Count Goltz. It was ratified on July 12,1807.

The Franco-Russian alliance contracted at Tilsit is of such import that a close analysis of all its stages is necessary. To begin with, the motives must be found which influenced both Alexander and Napoleon to sign a peace and alliance. Secondly, a careful study of the various articles and their implications is important because these articles not only represent rules by which the future French and Russian policies are governed, but contain in themselves the seed for the ultimate war between the two countries. In the last instance, the immediate events following the Tilsit meeting will be scrutinized.

The basis for the armistice and treaty at Tilsit can be found after

the battle of Eylau when the French army suffered its first major setback
on February 8,1807. Albert Vandal logically draws the conclusion that Napoleon,
after losing thousands of his soldiers and officers, must have changed his
impressions and opinions regarding the Russians and began to appreciate Russia
at her own true value, even as a potential ally against his primary enemy -
England.[3] In fact, on March 14, Napoleon wrote to Talleyrand

> I am of the opinion that an alliance with Russia
> would be very advantageous, if the idea was not
> fantastic.[4]

Napoleon ordered negotiations to be started with the Russian
commander, Benningsen, who, however, cut them short by replying that his task
was to fight and not to negotiate.[5]

Both France and Russia had approached Austria to win this country
over to their side. Austria, geographically situated between the warring parties,
offered to mediate between them. Czar Alexander, however, opted once more to
organize an effective coalition against Napoleon and to continue the war. On
April 26, he met with the King and Queen of Prussia at Bartenstein where he
signed a new convention between Russia and Prussia. Besides promising Prussia
the return of all the provinces she lost since 1805 (Article IV), the most
significant stipulation was in Article XV under which both nations undertook
that one would not lay down her arms without the other or sign peace indepen-
dently of each other.[6]

The combined forces of Russia and Prussia, comprising some 88,000 men,
met Napoleon's forces of some 150,000 men at Friedland for a decisive battle
on June 14. The combined Russian and Prussian troops were defeated and
Bennigsen wrote a letter to Czar Alexander on June 15 advising him "to begin
some negotiations for peace, if only to gain time and repair our losses."[7]

It was now Alexander's turn to ask for negotiations to be started;
his army was decomated and his counsellors and ministers, even those who were
most hostile against France, advised the Emperor to sue for peace.[8] Alexander
sent Prince Lobanov-Rostovsky to arrange for an armistice; on June 22 when
Napoleon dined with this emissary of the Czar he made the remark that the
Vistula ought to be the frontier of Russia and the dividing line of the
spheres of interest.[9] On June 25 Lobanov-Rostovsky returned to the French

headquarters with a letter from Czar Alexander in which the latter wrote
that only an alliance between France and Russia would guarantee the happiness
and peace of the world, and that a new political system had to be established.
He added that he could easily come to an understanding with Napoleon, "provided
we negoatiate without intermediaries."[10] Arrangements were accordingly made
for the two Emperors to meet on a raft on the Niemen River. Napoleon was
charmed with the Czar. He wrote to Josephine on June 25:

> I have just seen the Emperor Alexander and have been
> very pleased with him. He is a handsome, good young
> Emperor, and is more intelligent than is commonly
> believed.[11]

Napoleon's kindness towards Alexander was not exaggerated; he received
him with a refined artfulness and, as the Czar told King William of Prussia
after the first interview, Napoleon was "reserved, cold, but polite."[12]

Napoleon's effect upon Alexander must have been great. On June 7
the Czar wrote to his sister, the Grand-Duchess Catherine:

> What do you think ? . . . I ! passing my days with
> Bonaparte, remaining for whole hours alone with him.[13]

Alexander's enthusiasm was not shared by Catherine who replied with
a sentiment shared by most of her compatriots, that, as far as she was concerned,
the Tilsit peace was no peace . . .

> unless we secure great aquisitions on the Vistula and
> the Danube. For without these we shall have nothing but
> shame for fraternizing with a man against whom we have
> rightly raised our voices in condemnation, and there
> will be not the smallest real gain or honor for Russia
> in return.[14]

Alexander also told Napoleon's envoy in St.Petersburg, Savary,
about his first impression when he met the Emperor of the French at Tilsit:

> I have never been so prejudiced against anybody as
> against him,but after three-quarters of an hour of
> conversation with him, it all passed like a dream.[15]

Vandal, quoting from Hardenberg's *Memoires*, describes how the two
Emperors continued to meet in greatest intimacy and privacy; "I will be your
secretary," Napoleon told Alexander, "and you will be mine."[16] They conferred
together, attended parades, visited each other's camps, conversing not only
about Europe's future, but also about various ideologies.[17]

The first points of discussion were settled without difficulties after Alexander agreed to recognize all conquests and creations of his new ally prior to the war of 1806, such as stipulated under Article XV. There remained three outstanding problems to be settled: the fate of Prussia, the measures against England, and the question of Turkey.

Prussia

It might be asserted that, by signing a peace treaty with France, Alexander broke the convention of Bartenstein. Alexander must have been conscious of this violation and he took it upon himself to conduct the negotiation in the interest of Prussia at Tilsit. It was also he who secured the concessions Napoleon made to Prussia.

Napoleon's first plan was to detach Silesia away from Prussia and give the same to a French prince.[18] Frederick William, in an interview with Napoleon on July 1, appealed to the Emperor against this decision, but Napoleon remained adamant, declaring, "I must have that province for the King of Saxony, who needs a free line of communication between Saxony and the Duchy of Warsaw.[19]

No history of the fate of Prussia at that time would be complete if an account is not given of the scheme worked out by the Prussian minister Hardenberg, who, to save his country, proposed a plan which should satisfy both Russia and France. This plan was approved by Frederick William and submitted to Alexander as a basis for his discussions with Napoleon. Under Hardenberg's scheme Russia should receive part of the Principalities, Bulgaria and Rumelia; Austria should acquire Dalmatia together with Serbia and Bosnia; France should get Greece and the Ionian Islands.[20] Alexander did not submit Hardenberg's plan to Napoleon, but it is evident that he did also not agree to the dismemberment of Prussia and would not even accept Poland at this price.[21]

Napoleon finally did drop his demand for Silesia, but, in compensation, he made further demands of South Prussia and New East Prussia (i.e. the Polish Provinces) as well as the Prussian provinces beyond the Elbe, though he was willing to grant the restoration of some 600,000 souls in different districts there.[22] In connection with this grant Napoleon wrote Alexander on July 3:

> In consenting today to give the King of Prussia
> compensation on the left of the Elbe . . . the
> Emperor Napoleon desires Russia to receive the
> limit of the Niemen.[23]

Alexander replied on July 4:

> My demands are moderate, they are disinterested,
> since I only plead the cause of an unfortunate ally.[24]

On the same day Napoleon wrote a letter to the Czar referring to
the latter's suggestion -

> To call Prince Jerome to the throne of Saxony and
> Warsaw would in an instant overthrow all our good
> relations . . . The policy of Emperor Napoleon is
> that his immediate influence does not extend the
> Elbe, and he adopted this policy because it is the
> only one which can agree with the system of sincere
> and constant friendship he wishes to establish with
> the great empire of the North.[25]

Napoleon's principal aim was to contain Prussia between the Elbe and
the Niemen. Alexander had accepted the increase of territory for Russia at the
expense of Prussia; Prussia was to be compensated partly in Poland and partly
by a section of Saxon territory taken from the right bank of the Elbe. Napoleon
thus withdrew his previous offer /see above/. Alexander was not satisfied and,
two days later, Napoleon proposed a "mezzo-termine" on all points. To the
Russian demand of 200,000 souls to the left of the Elbe for Prussia, Napoleon
made a counterproposal which was embodied in Article V of the Secret Treaty
of Tilsit:

> If Hanover, at the conclusion of peace with England,
> comes to be joined to the Kingdom of Westphalia, then
> lands on the left of the Elbe to the extent of three
> to four thousand souls will be restored to the King of
> Prussia.

Considering, however, that Article VII of the Treaty of Alliance
stipulated that Hanover should be restored to England of the British Government accepted Napoleon's terms, this "mezzo-termine" was anything but a success
for Alexander and his efforts on behalf of Prussia.

On July 6 Napoleon wrote a letter to the Czar in which he granted him
his desire that Prussia should have an increase in her Polish territories, so
that she had a continuity of possession between Berlin and Koenigsberg - "as
to the exchange of Memel for a portion of Saxony, that does not create any
difficulty."[26]

On the same day Alexander had also written a letter to Napoleon
in which he states:

> I have shown the Emperor Napoleon that I was ready
> to acquiesce in his plans and cede the Ionian Islands
> and Cattaro, but he will recall at the same time
> how pronounced was my wish to use these cessions for
> the amelioration of the lot of an unhappy ally.[27]

In this letter Alexander asks for a restoration of 200,000 souls
on the left of the Elbe, including the Altmark and the rest of Magdeburg and
Halberstadt, "which the Emperor himself admits that he promised me."

Alexander fought every step of the way to retain as much territory
for Prussia as possible, but Napoleon remained adamant, especially in the
general principle that Prussia should under no circumstances be left wider
than fifty leagues along a line running from Koenigsberg to Berlin.[28]

The Czar kept the Prussian Court informed of all negotiations, and,
at a crucial moment, Queen Louise of Prussia called upon Napoleon in person.
Napoleon refused to discuss politics with the Queen. On the evening of July 8
he dined with her and afterwards wrote to Josephine:

> The Queen is really charming;she is full of cocquetterie
> for me; but do not be jealous; I am an oil-cloth over
> which all that can flow. It would cost me too much to
> play the lover.[29]

In his treaty with Russia, Napoleon consented to list the names of
the Prussian territories he was pledging himself to evacuate, as well as
all territorial changes (Articles IV,V,VI,VII,VIII,X, XI, XII of the Peace
Treaty), "out of special deference to His Majesty the Emperor of All the
Russians," (Article IV of the Peace Treaty).

According to Article V of the Peace Treaty, the provinces which
were on January 1,1772, part of the ancient Kingdom of Poland, and which
have passed during various times under Prussian domination, will be incorporated under the title of Duchy of Warsaw.

All these articles are also contained in the separate Treaty
Napoleon made with Prussia, but the evacuation of French troops was delayed
until the fulfillment of a separate Convention signed at Koenigsberg on July 12,
1807.[30] In Article II of this Convention the dates of evacuation are listed
for the various Prussian cities in which French garrisons were stationed, as

well as for the entire territories occupied by the French army. The evacuation, however, was dependent on and subject to the fulfilment of the payment of contributions which were imposed by France (Article IV). The demanded contribution amounted to 154 million Francs, a sum which the King of Prussia could not possibly raise from or in his impoverished and decimated kingdom. Frederick William requested in July a decrease of this sum and made a counterproposal of 30 million Francs, payable within three years. This was not acceptable to Napoleon who remained adamant, demanding the original sum stipulated.[31]

The question of the evacuation of Prussia was an important diplomatic victory for Napoleon. Though Alexander bound himself in the Treaty of Tilsit to evacuate Wallachia and Moldavia,[32] Napoleon was able to leave the question of the evacuation of Prussia to a subsequent convention. This is important as can be seen from a letter by the French Foreign Minister Champagny[33] to Savary on November 8, 1807:

> The Emperor Alexander will recall that it was the intention
> that this term was not fixed for the Prussian provinces
> as it was for Wallachia and Moldavia; it was with the view
> of not losing all the chances that the future might offer,
> and so that we might be ready for any opportunity. We limited
> ourselves therefore to saying that a convention would deter-
> mine this period. The convention was not made between France
> and Russia; therefore Russia has nothing more to require
> from France.[34]

It is evident from this letter that the execution of the Convention of Koenigsberg was a matter in which, according to Napoleon's interpretation, the Czar had no right to interfere. By demanding a very large financial indemnity from Prussia, Napoleon indefinitely delayed the evacuation of his forces and circumvented thereby also the treaties he had with Prussia and Russia. Prussia thus lost all her freedom of action and was bound to the policy of France; the continuation of a French occupation of Prussia, however, was to become a bargaining point of major importance in the future relations between France and Russia.

The Measures Against England

The articles concerning England give a good indication of the full force and tremendous potentialities of the new Franco-Russian alliance against a common enemy. In Article XIII of the Peace Treaty -

> H.M.Emperor Napoleon accepts the mediation of H.M.
> Emperor of all the Russians to negotiate and conclude
> a definite peace between France and England, under
> the condition that England will accept such mediation
> one month after the ratification of the present treaty.

What was expected from England is clearly stated in Article IV of
the Treaty of Alliance:

> . . . to respect the flags of all nations upon the
> seas and restore all conquests she made against France
> and her allies since 1805. If by December 1 England
> still remained obstinate, Russia is to make common
> cause with France and declare war.

Napoleon must have promised himself good results against England
from this alliance. On July 6 he wrote to Alexander:

> . . . if England does not make peace before November,
> she will certainly make it when, at that time, she
> will know your Majesty's intentions and will see the
> crisis which is in preparation to close the entire
> Continent to her.[35]

Russia's minister in London, Maximilian Alopeus, was not informed of
the details concerning the Treaties of Tilsit; he was merely instructed to
announce the conclusion of the treaties and offer of mediation; for the rest
he was as much in the dark as Canning, the British Foreign Minister.[36]

The news concerning Tilsit was alarming for England. Budberg, the
Russian minister of foreign relations, avoided carefully the British ambassador
to Russia, Leveson-Gower, who had been sent to the Czar in Poland, and
merely informed him in a letter of June 30 that there has been a change of
policy. "The conduct which has been pursued by your government of late," wrote
Budberg, is calculated completely to justify the determination which the Czar
has just taken."[37] Leveson-Gower saw in the Tilsit treaties great dangers for
his country -

> . . . the most deadly blows are aiming at the cery
> existence of the country; for be assured that the
> dangers which threaten England at this moment infini-
> tely exceed what we ever before apprehended.[38]

On August 5 Canning gave his answer to the Russian peace proposals
in a letter to Alopeus:

> His Majesty trusts that the character of the Treaty
> of Tilsit and of the principles upon which France
> is represented as being ready to negotiate, may be
> found to be such as to afford to His Majesty a just
> hope of the attainment of a secure and honorable
> peace.
>
> In that case His Majesty will readily avail himself
> of the Emperor of Russia's mediation.
>
> But until His Majesty shall have received these
> important and necessary communications it is obviously
> impossible that the undersigned should be authorized
> to return a more specific answer to the note presented
> by M. d'Alopeus.[39]

Czar Alaxnder proceeded very carefully at that time in order not to
give away any of the stipulations he agreed to at Tilsit. This caution was
based upon a very good reason: Russia's best fleet, used in the war against
Turkey in the Levant under Admiral Seniavin, was recalled and made its way
slowly northwards across the Mediterranean where it was at the mercy of
British warships. If the Tilsit stipulations were to be known in London, the
Russian fleet would be in great danger. This is confirmed in a letter from
Leveson-Gower to Canning on August 2, when the former in an official report
from St.Petersburg declares:

> It is with pain I inform you that everything I have
> heard and observed since I came here strongly confirms
> the apprehension . . . that the Emperor Alexander has
> Completely thrown himself into the hands of Bonaparte . . .
> but, whatever may be the ultimate intentions of this
> government, it appears that they are desirous of avoiding
> a quarrel with the Court of London, for the present at
> least, till the return of the fleet from the Mediterranean.[40]

Thus, while the Czar in the month of August was playing a delaying
game, the English Government for its own part was not anxious to hasten a
crisis either. Canning's instructions to Leveson-Gower on August 5 were "to
feign ignorance of what he only knew too well," and also to let no hint fall
that the British Government knew of the connivance of Russia in Napoleon's
maritime league.[41]

What Canning was referring to was England's intention to take
preventive measures in the Baltic. By its geographical position and its

well-equipped navy, Denmark was the target for a British naval expedition under
Admiral Gambier. Between September 2 and 5, the British fleet bombarded Copen-
hagen with such "terrible effect" that, on September 7 Denmark surrendered to
England its entire fleet. The duty of Leveson-Gower was to explain the Danish
expedition as directed against Napoleon and not intended as a threat to the
Cazr.[42]

It is at this juncture when a new personage must be introduced who
played a decisive part in the Anglo-Russian relations during the critical months
between August and November 1807.

One of the most popular figures among the Englishmen in St.Petersburg
was Sir Robert Wilson, a soldier and adventurer, popular in society, and an
avowed enemy of Napoleon. In one of his letters to Lord Malmesbury, Wilson
described how Alexander returned to St.Petersburg after Tilsit and how he found
opinion equally hostile against what had been done. The Czar's mother, the Dowager-
Empress, received him with the following rebuke: "You are young and you have time
to repent."[43] On August 18, Wilson had his first interview with the Czar, followed
by a private dinner on September 2. On September 20 he arrived in London where he
spread the tidings that the Tilsit Treaty was but a snare for Napoleon and a
"breath-space" for the Czar.[44] The intelligence brought by Wilson, whose reputation
stood high in every country except his own, was not taken seriously until
Leveson-Gower wrote to England that he shared Wilson's optimism.[45]

Under these circumstances Canning decided to send Wilson back to St.
Petersburg with instructions which were partly an admonition. Wilson was to
make it clear that "England does not wish to precipitate Russia into a war with
France by claiming preference for herself, but she requires an equality of consi-
deration which is necessary for Russia to preserve the station of an independent
power." Further, the British Government would be willing to gratify Russian
ambitions on many points; England was willing and prepared to recognize Russia
as "The Protectress of the North"; the British Government was further willing
to compel the surrender of the Ionian Islands by Napoleon in order that they might
be handed over to the Czar."[46]

Wilson arrived back in St.Petersburg on September 17. The value of the
British proposals was not thoroughly tested, for in the interval of Wilson's

absence the Czar had changed his minister of foreign relations; Budberg was succeeded by Count Nicholas Rumiantsev, a Gallophil, who had been one of the principal advisers of Catherine II. Wilson saw Rumiantsev on October 30 and the latter accepted the British proposals with a great deal of reserve.

Seeing that his mission had been in vain, Wilson, in connivance with Leveson-Gower, spread a pamphlet entitled "Reflections on the Peace of Tilsit" which contained bitter attacks upon Alexander and his policy. Savary, who called Wilson a "postillon d'intrigues et de corruptions,"[47] kept a close watch on the latter and managed to procure one of the pamphlets Wilson was distributing in the closed and intimate circle of the Russian nobility into which Savary had no access. The pamphlet was delivered to the Czar whose reaction was drastic as well as unexpected. A letter which Wilson had written to him remained unanswered. Instead, on November 7, the Russian Government broke off diplomatic relations with Great Britain and reaffirmed Russia's stand pertaining the maritime law contested in London.[48] On November 8, Wilson received orders to leave St.Petersburg. He arrived in London on December 2, informing Canning of Russia's step before the Russian courier reached England. As a result of his speed, the Russian frigate _Sperknei_ was seized before it had the opportunity of leaving English waters.[49]

Thus Russia, according to the stipulation of Tilsit, declared a state of war with England, as much as a whole month before the date set by the treaty. This, in turn, was exploited as a diplomatic weapon by Alexander in his demands on Napoleon.[50] From a military point of view the Anglo-Russian hostilities were negligible; from an economic point of view they were disastrous for Russia.

The Turkish Question

The articles both of the Peace Treaty and the Treaty of Alliance concerning Turkey show a remarkable correlation with those dealing with England. Yet, there is one decisive difference.

Alexander made definite promises both with regard to the nature of his negotiations with England as well as in case if these negotiations should fail. Napoleon, on the other hand, only in vague terms undertook to mediate between Russia and Turkey. Moreover, according to Article VIII of the Treaty of Alliance,

France promised . . .

> to make common cause with Russia against the Ottoman
> Porte, and the two contracting parties will agree to
> liberate all the provinces of the Ottoman Empire in
> Europe, with the exception of Constantinople and the
> province of Rumelia, from the yoke and vexations of
> the Turks.

During the meeting at Tilsit between the two Emprerors, Napoleon showed
to the Czar dispatches he had received from his ambassador in Constantinople,
Comte Horace Sebastiani. In these dispatches Sebastiani reported insurrection
against Sultan Selim. "It is a degree of Providence," Napoleon commented, "which
tells me that the Turkish Empire can no longer exists."[51] To Talleyrand he wrote:

> My system concerning Turkey is wavering and is about to
> fall, but still I have not made a decision yet.[52]

According to Article XXII of the Peace Treaty, Alexander promised to
evacuate the Principalities,[53] but Napoleon told him verbally that he did not
attach too great a value to the execution of this clause and would not insist
with force on a withdrawal of the Muscovite troops.[54]

Simultaneously with Russia's action against England, Napoleon sent a
French officer, Adjutant-Commander Guilleminot, to the Russian headquarters in
Wallachia to negotiate for an armistice between Russia and Turkey. Such an armistice was concluded on August 4 at Slobodzia. In Article III of this armistice the
conditions for an evacuation of Moldavia and Wallachia by the Russians are
repeated as in Article XXII of the Peace Treaty of Tilsit.[55]

Remembering probably Napoleon's verbal statements at Tilsit, Alexander
refused to ratify this armistice. Most likely in refusing to ratify this armistice and evacuate the Principalities, the Czar was motivated by the situation of
Prussia. The French forces had not evacuated Prussia, hence he felt under no
obligation to evacuate the Principalities. These two problems became inextricably
tangled and resulted in the near future in a renewed meeting between the two
Emperors.

On November 1, Napoleon had exchanged his envoy in St.Petersburg for
his new ambassador, Armand-Augustin-Louis de Caulaincourt. Napoleon felt that
he had to clarify his position concerning Prussia, especially after Alexander's
various hints to Savary about his expectations in Turkey after the declaration
of war against England.[56]

Napoleon sent a long instruction to Caulaincourt on November 12 in which he gave the latter explicit details for his negotiations with the Czar. Napoleon declared that he would not refuse such a concession (the non-evacuation of the Principalities) for the sake and with the desire to gratify an ally who at the same time was also his friend. However, the Tilsit Treaty could not be modified to the exclusive advantage of one party; the infraction allowed to Russia must also allow an infraction profitable for France. Reason, justice, and prudence do not allow the French Emperor to take another point of view, and no obstacle can stop him from this.[57]

Napoleon obviously did not see the correlation between Russia's demands in the Principalities with his own stand in Prussia. Having imposed upon Prussia a contribution so enormous that the country could not pay it, Napoleon used this non-payment as the reason for not evacuating Silesia.[58] Napoleon obviously thought he had a legal justification to remain in Prussia and Russia could not regard the non-evacuation of Wallachia and Moldavia as a compensation for his occupation of Prussia. On the other hand, Alexander informed Caulaincourt that there could be no question of a dismemberment of Prussia serving as compensation to France for Russia's conquests in Turkey.[59] Thus, barely six months from the outset of the alliance, an impasse had been reached which soon was growing into a crisis.

When Napoleon realized that Russia would never agree to his non-evacuation of Prussia in return for the Principalities, a new plan was developed in his mind in which both Russia and France could be satisfied. This plan envisaged a partition of Turkey.

On February 2,1808, Napoleon wrote a long letter to the Czar in which he declared that, since negotiations with England had failed, it was only by "great and vast measures that peace could be attained." Russia should proceed actively against Sweden in the North, while an army of fifty thousand Russians, Frenchmen, and perhaps Austrians, should advance towards India; the French coming from Dalmatia and the Russians from the Danube. For such a vast project Napoleon would not refuse any stipulation as preamble, but, as he states in his letter, "the interests of our two States must be combined and balanced." This can only be done in a meeting with the Czar, or decided in a serious conference between Caulaincourt and Rumiantsev. Of Tolstoi, the Czar's ambassador in Paris, Napoleon said he is a "good man, but he is filled with prejudice and suspicions against

France, and as far from the spirit of Tilsit and the new position in which
the close friendship between Your Majesty and me has placed us in the universe."
Everything could be settled before March 15 and by May 1 and the united forces
could be in Asia. Napoleon concludes:

> The work of Tilsit will decide the fate of the world; let
> us realize that the era for great changes and great events
> has arrived.[60]

Vandal correctly concludes that this letter was nothing more than a
vast illusion to be waved in front of the Czar's eyes, while behind this bluff
Napoleon intended to pursue his designs in Spain, the only ones with which he
was seriously concerned at that particular time. Once the Spanish question had
been resolved, Russia and Europe could be placed before a fait accompli and
Napoleon would withdraw his offers and allow the mirage, so splendidly evoked,
to disappear.[61]

The Russian and Prussian issues, in addition to certain other vital
questions, were the main stumbling block to the alliance of Russia and France
contracted in Article I of the Treaty of Alliance which stipulated that -

> H.M.the Emperor of France, King of Italy, and H.M. the
> Emperor of All the Russias engage themselves to make
> common cause be it on land or sea, and in all wars in
> which France and Russia will of necessity be implicated
> or will have to wage against all the force of Europe.

With Russia as ally, Napoleon hoped to be able to isolate Europe
completely from England. With the Continent shut to British merchandise, it could
be easy to assume that a panic would get hold of England, and, with all the
consequences, force the British Government to sue for peace. The European states
had to abide by Napoleon's commands and wishes, but the various declarations
of war remained little more than just fiction.

-16-

N O T E S

1. All articles of the Peace Treaty and the Treaty of Alliance are printed in full by A.Vandal in his Napoleon et Alexandre Ier, Vol.I, Appendix I, pp.500-507, after the text published by De Clerq and conserved in the Archives of the French Foreign Ministry.

2. G.F.Martens. Recueil des Principaux Traités de l'Europe, Vol.VIII,pp.661-668.

3. A.Vandal. Op.cit., p.33

4. (C)orrespondence de (N)apoleon Ier, Vol.XV, 12028.

5. A.Lobanov-Rostovsky. Russia and Europe 1789-1825, Ch.VI, p.152.

6. All articles of the Treaty of Bartenstein are given in G.F.de Martens, Op. cit., pp.606-612.

7. Bennigsen to Alexander in Sbornik, LXXXIX, p.10, printed in H.Butterfield's The Peace Tactics of Napoleon 1806-8, Appendix A, p.361.

8. A.Vandal. Op.cit., p.50

9. Tatischeff. Nouvelle Revue (June 1,1890), quoted in A.Vandal, Op.cit., p.52.

10. Ibid.

11. C.N., Vol. XV, 12825.

12. King Frederick William to Queen Louise, 25th June 1807, quoted in H.Butterfielc Op.cit., Book III, Ch.III, p.256.

13. Grand Duke Nicholas Mikhailovitch. Correspondence d'Alexandre Ier avec la Granc Duchess Catherine, quoted in H.Butterfield, Op.cit., p.264.

14. Ibid., p.264.

15. Savary's report from October 9,1807, quoted in A.Vandal, Op.cit.,Ch.I, p.81.

16. Hardenberg. Denkwuerdikeiten, Vol.III, p.490, quoted in A.Vandal, Op.cit., Ch.I, p.81.

17. A.Vandal. Op.cit., Ch.I, p.84, quoting from Napoleon's Memorial by Las Cases, March 10-12,1816.

18. Frederick William to Queen Louise, June 30,1807. See Paul Bailleu, "Die Verhandlungen in Tilsit - Briefwechsel König Friedrich Wilhelm's III und der Königin Luise," Deutsche Rundschau, Vol. CX, p.110.

19. As told to Princess Anton Radziwill by Czar Alexander, quoted in H.Butterfield, Op.cit., Book III,Ch.II, p.235.

20. Hardenberg, Op.cit.,III, pp.461-3, quoted in A.Vandal, Op.cit.,Ch.I, p.71.

21. H.Butterfield, Op.cit.,Appendix C. p.373, quoting a report from De Bray in Handelsman, Napoleon et la Pologne (1909), p.128.

22. Paul Bailleu, Op.cit. in Deutsche Rundschau, CX, p.110, citing a letter from Frederick William to Queen Luise, June 30,1807.

23. Sbornik LXXXVIII, pp.57-8, in H.Butterfield, Op.cit., p.374.

24. Ibid, p.376.

25. C.N., XV, 12849.

26. C.N., XV, 12862.

27. Sbornik LXXXVIII, pp.70-2, in H.Butterfield, Op.cit., Appendix C, p.377.

28. C.N., XV, 12863 /N.B. 1 league equals 3 miles or 4.83 kms.)

29. C.N., XV, 12875

30. All articles of this convention are given in G.F.de Martens, Op.cit.,pp.668-670.

31. L.von Ranke. Hardenberg, Vol.III, Ch.IV, p.81.

32. Cp. page 1.

33. Talleyrand had given up his position as Foreign Minister after his elevation to Prince of Benevento following the Tilsit meeting.

34. Sbornik LXXXVIII, p.212, quoted in H.Butterfield, Op.cit., p.380.

35. C.N., XV, 12865.

36. H.Butterfield, Op.cit.,Book IV, Ch.II, pp.286-7, also footnote on p.287.

37. Sbornik LXXXIX, p.44, quoted in H.Butterfield, Op.cit., p.287.

38. Private correspondence of Lord G.Leveson-Gower, II, 272, quoted in H. Butterfield, Op.cit., pp.287-8.

39. Parliamentary Debates, X, cols.114-5, in H.Butterfield, Op.cit., p.289.

40. Quoted in H.Butterfield, Op.cit., p.289.

41. Ibid., pp.290-1.

42. Canning to G.Leveson-Gower, August 13,1807, quoted in H.Butterfield, Op.cit., p.291.

43. Malmesbury, Letters, Vol.II, p.29, quoted in G.Costigan, Sir Robert Wilson, Ch.II, p.41.

44. Ibid.

45. Malmesbury, Op.cit., p.50, in Costigan, Op.cit., p.43.

46. Draft of instructions from Mr.Canning to Sir Robert Wilson (n.d.),quoted in G.Costigan, Op.cit., p.44.

47. Savary's letter to Napoleon, October 21,1807, quoted in A.Vandal, Op.cit., Ch.III, p.152.

48. The full text of the Russian declaration of war is given in G.F.de Martens, Op.cit., pp.706-710.

49. G.Costigan, Op.cit., Ch.II, p.48.

50. Cp.Ibid, p.2.

51. Savary's report of November 4,1807, quoted in A.Vandal, Op.cit., Ch.I, p.73.

52. C.N., XV, 12886 (July 9,1807).

53. Cp, p.1.

54. This verbal engagement is mentioned in Alexander's instructions to Tolstoi: footnote in A.Vandal, Op.cit., Ch.I, p.105.

55. The full text of this armistice is given in G.F.de Martens, Op.cit.,pp.689-692

56. Savary's report of November 4,1807, quoted in A.Vandal, Op.cit.,Ch.III,p.169.

57. Quoted by A.Vandal, Op.cit., Appendix II, pp.508-513.

58. Cp. pp. 6-8.

59. Caulaincourt's report of December 23,1807, in A.Vandal, Op.cit., Ch.V,p.207.

60. C.N., not numbered, XVI, p.498, also quoted in A.Vandal, Op.cit., Ch.VII, pp.242-4.

61. A.Vandal, Op.cit., Ch.VII, p.245.

THE ERFURT CONVENTION

In March 1808 the Spanish crisis broke out and alrming news reached Napoleon from Vienna that Austria was feverishly re-arming. Napoleon suspected that the Austrian re-armament was intended to admit Austria as a third partner in the arrangement of Tilsit. With this in mind, Napoleon confronted the Austrian ambassador in Paris, Metternich, adding -

> . . . what can you do against France and Russia united ?
> And the first war with Austria will be a war to the death;
> you must either come to Paris, or I must make a conquest
> of your kingdom. Your armaments are equally displeasing
> to St.Petersburg. Do you know how this will end ? The
> Emperor Alexander will tell you that he desires you to
> stop, and you will do it; and then it will no longer be
> you on whom I shall depend for maintainance of tranquility
> in Europe; it will be Russia. I shall not submit to you
> the future arrangements of many questions in which you are
> interested; I shall treat solely with Russia, and you will
> only be spectators.[1]

Faced with a Spanish insurrection and a possible war with Austria, the proposed expedition to India[2] had by necessity become of minor importance; Russia's help against a possible war with Austria now became a major issue. In a note to Talleyrand, Napoleon expressed his feelings about the need for a renewed understanding with Alexander -

> The fate of Europe and of the world, the future of
> political power and perhaps of European civilization
> depends on it.[3]

As for Russia, her war with Sweden was dragging on and the aid Napoleon had promised was not forthcoming; Bernadotte, Napoleon's general sent to succur the Russians, stopped at the coats of Holstein.

Alexander considered that by his wars with England and Sweden he had amply fulfilled the stipulations of Tilsit, whereas France had not declared war on Turkey and had repeaid him with nothing more than empty schemes. The withdrawal of forces from Prussia was only undertaken because these troops were needed in Spain, and even then this withdrawal was far from complete. Three fortresses, Stettin, Glogau, and Kuestrin, remained occupied by French troops. Further, Napoleon had reinforced his troops in the Duchy of Warsaw. The Prussia issue was extremely important to Alexander and at would be stressed, more than any other, at their next meeting.[4]

This next meeting took place at Erfurt in Germany. The Conference
began on September 28,1808, and ended on October 12,1808.

The Czar proved himself a most stubborn negotiator. Napoleon observed
to Caulaincourt that Alexander was "stubborn like a mule."[5] Alexander's obstinacy
was most evident in connection with the evacuation of Prussia by French troops.
Napoleon considered that he needed Prussia as a flank against Austria and his
argument against the Czar's insistence was that -

> . . . the prolonged stay of a few troops in Prussia
> cannot disquiet Russia when I pull all my forces from
> Germany in order to bring them to the Peninsula. This
> measure proves my confidence in you; have the same in
> me and do not destroy by unwarranted worries the good
> effect of our arrangement. Should you insist, I must
> give in, but then I would prefer to abandon my affairs
> in Spain and settle immediately my quarrel with Austria.
> If I evacuate the places on the Oder, you should evacuate
> those on the Danube. It is in your interest to remain
> there as you can be certain to receive Wallachia and
> Moldavia . . . The occupation I hold is thus more
> in your interest than in mine. You will immediately
> be able to reap the advantages, while I have nothing
> to expect.[6]

Napoleon further appealed to the Czar to keep up the alliance "at a
time when we will take steps to bring England to peace" as well as for the
reason that "we appear united and strong in the eyes of our common enemies."[7]

Caulaincourt in his Memoirs expresses the opinion that Napoleon was
prepared at Erfurt to make sacrifices, such as giving Russia a free hand with
regard to the Danube Principalities, in order to maintain the peace.

Alexander's obstinacy at Erfurt was greatly influenced by the man who
had been entrusted with the handling of France's external relations ever since
the days of the Directory. Talleyrand, a diplomat of the old school, in the words
of Metternich -

> . . . since the campaigns of 1805 opposed with all his
> influence, as Minister of Foreign Affairs, the destruc-
> tive plans of Napoleon - a subordinate influence as to
> the political point of view of the Emperor, but powerful
> in the practical means of execution. Two men in France
> hold at this moment the first rank in opinions and influ-
> ence - M.de Talleyrand and M.Fouché.[8]

The first day of his arrival at Erfurt, Talleyrand presented himself
to Alexander to whom he said:

> Sire, what are you going to do here ? It rests
> with you to save Europe, and you can only accom-
> plish this by resisting Napoleon. The French
> people are civilized, its Sovereign is not; the
> Sovereign of Russia is civilized, and his people
> are not; it is therefore for the Sovereign of
> Russia to be allied to the French people.[9]

Talleyrand's words not only encouraged Alexander to oppose Napoleon,

his further statements to Metternich in Paris inspired the latter to advise

his Court to try for a reproachment with Russia, for, in Talleyrand's view,

"it depends on you and on your ambassador at St.Petersburg, to renew the

intimate relations with Russia. It is this alliance alone which can save to

Europe the remnants of her independence."[10] Talleyrand further informed

Metternich that Caulaincourt was entirely devoted to his political system and is

"instructed in a way to second all the steps of Prince Schwarzenberg (the

Austrian ambassador at St.Petersburg). The Powers which are in a position to

make a stand against Napoleon must combine and bar the way to his insatiable

ambition; it is to the interest of France herself that they should do so. The

cause of Napoleon is no longer that of France; Europe itself can only be saved

by the closest cooperation between Austria and Russia."[11]

How much the Czar was impressed by Talleyrand's words can be seen

from his letter to Rumiantsev on December 8,1808:

> . , . since the most enlightened and wise men of
> France themselves suspect and disapprove the imperial
> policy, is it for me to approve an ambition which
> knows no limits and to help it to break all obstacles ?[12]

While the two Emperors discussed general principles, their ministers,

Talleyrand for France and Rumiantsev for Russia, worked out the details of the

Convention which was ratified on October 12,1808.

The Convention[13] stipulated that a joint offer of peace should be made

to England and that the two powers would act jointly in negotiations which may

result from this offer. In Articles I-III France and Russia respectively guaran-

teed their mutual conquests accomplished since Tilsit, and each power retained

whatever it had occupied (Article IV). In Articles V,VI,VII and VIII France

accepted the annexation by Russia of Finland, Wallachia, and Moldavia. France

further promised to obtain recognition of these annexations from England in

the coming negotiations with that power. In Article IX Russia obtained the right to negotiate directly with Turkey without French interference or mediation, promising in return not to set her forces in action in the Danubian region before January 1,1809. Should Austria attack Russia, France would come to the aid of her ally, and, conversely, Russia would aid France in the event of a war with Austria (Article X). A new meeting between the Emperors would be arranged within a year in the event of failure of the peace negotiations, and the contracting parties also pledged themselves to respect and guarantee the remaining possessions of the Turkish Empire (Articles XII - XVI).

By the Erfurt Convention Napoleon hoped to bring Europe to a position in which, according to the Tilsit arrangement, it should have been by the beginning of 1808 - united against England under French leadership. Napoleon's position has, however, deteriorated since Tilsit; the Spanish insurrection, on one side, and the Austrian re-armament on the other, delayed the all-out war against England and the solution of these two problems became a matter of the utmost priority. Consequently, and to ensure Alexander's cooperation in case of a war with Austria, Napoleon showed himself willing to make a one-sided concession. This concession was limited to the Danubian Principalities. The Erfurt Convention was thus a re-affirmation of the Tilsit Agreement implemented in its intentions not only against England, but also against Austria.

The was another incentive which actuated Napoleon's renewed meeting with the Czar at Erfurt. This incentive was a personal matter to Napoleon which, however, he did not want to broach to Alexander, entrusting it rather to his two ministers, Talleyrand and Caulaincourt. Napoleon's intention was that Talleyrand should, in the course of a conversation with Alexander, suggest the desirability of a remarriage by Napoleon "in order to consolidate his work and ensure the continuation of his dynasty."[14] Napoleon confirmed this plan to Caulaincourt at Erfurt, adding -

> This is to see if Alexander is really one of my friends and if he takes a true interest in the welfare of France.[15]

Napoleon inquired with Caulaincourt about the Russian Grand-Duchesses and the latter informed him that there was only one of marriageable age, but that one would never agree to changing her religion.

Talleyrand, who favored an Austrian alliance, realized the delicacy of the situation and considered it wiser to allow Cauliancourt to take the initiative.

Three months after the Erfurt Convention, the Grand-Duchess Catherine, who was closest to Alexander and who alone of his sister was old enough to marry, was engaged to the Duke of Oldenburg. The Czar's youngest sister, the Grand-Duchess Anne, was only fourteen years of age, a fact which was subsequently made the ostensible pretext for rejecting Napoleon's offer of marriage.

Talleyrand's and Caulaincourt's efforts at Erfurt to dissuade Napoleon from declaring war on Austria in the end proved unsuccessful. Austria, giving way to popular feelings, decided to declare war against France herself. The Austrian decision. no doubt, was also strongly inspired upon the second Memorandum which Metternich drew up in Vienna on December 4,1808. In this Memorandum, Metternich attempted to show how much the French army was weakened in Europe owing to the war in Spain and what the maximum force would or could be which Napoleon could muster to face the Austrian forces.[16]

N O T E S

1. Metternich to Stadion on August 17,1808, in Metternich, II, No.114,p.238.

2. Cp.Chapter I, p.14.

3. A.Vandal, Napoleon et Alexandre Ier, quotation from the Archives of the Foreign Ministry (not dated), I, Ch.XII, p.407.

4. This account follows the opinions of A.Lobanov Rostovsky, Russia and Europe, 1789-1825, pp.178-80, and A.Vandal, Op.cit., pp.392-407.

5. Reports of his conversation with Napoleon at Erfurt by Caulaincourt in his Memoires, I.,p.273.

6. Conversation between Napoleon and Alexander quoted by Caulaincourt, Op.cit.,p.2

7. Ibid., pp.272-3.

8. From the Memorandum drawn up by Metternich in Vienna, December 4,1808, in Metternich, Op.cit., No.127, pp.289-300.

9. Ibid.

10. Ibid.

11. Ibid.

12. Quoted in A.Vandal, Op.cit., p.423.

13. All articles of the Erfurt Convention (Convention D'Alliance) are contained in the (C)orrespondence de (N)apoleon Ier, Vol.XVII, 14372.

14. E.Dard, Napoleon and Talleyrand, Ch.XI, pp.188-9.

15. Caulaincourt, Op.cit., p.274.

16. Metternich, Op.cit., No.128, pp.301-8.

THE FRANCO-RUSSIAN RELATIONS DURING THE WAR

OF 1809

AND THE AUSTRIAN MARRIAGE

On January 23,1809, Napoleon returned to Paris from Spain preoccupied with the turn of events taking place in Austria where the armaments and conscription had reached their peak. On January 28 he dismissed Talleyrand. Alexander, too, made a change; Tolstoi's place as ambassador to France was taken by Prince Kurakin.

Rumiantsev, the Czar's foreign minister was in Paris where, together with Champagny, he was to conduct negotiations for a peace with England. Napoleon confided his rage and aims against Austria to Rumiantsev, stating that what Austria wanted was "a slap in the face, and I will give it to her on both cheeks, and you will see how she will thank me and ask for orders from me about what she has to do."[1] Metternich, also in Paris, observed how Rumiantsev attempted to calm Napoleon and continued his efforts to persuade him against a war with Austria.[2] Rumiantsev's role as peacemaker was not crowned with success; in Metternich's words, he was "always vacillating, sometimes confident and sometimes discouraged. His desire of achieving a maritime peace has not been any more successful than, unfortunately, his attempts to preserve the continental peace."[3]

As the crisis was approaching, Champagny continued sending urgent dispatches to Caulaincourt, drawing the ambasaador's attention to the urgent need for prompt action against Austria. On March 4 Napoleon instructed Champagny to send a courier to St.Petersburg with a transcript of his conversation with Metternich. Besides, the Czar should be informed that he had reunited all the troops of the Confederation of the Rhine because "it is absolutely necessary to get out of this situation; it seems Austria has ordered her troops to march; I count upon the Emperor's promise to march from his side; finally, peace with England is not feasible until the Continent is not pacified."[4]

On April 9, the Austrian army crossed into Bavaria beginning thus her war against France. Six days later, St.Petersburg received the news of this Austrian move. The Czar made it known that he would recall his ambassador from Vienna as well as dismiss Schwarzenberg from Russia. To Napoleon he wrote:

> Your Majesty can count on me; my means are not great,
> having already two wars on hand, but all what is
> possible will be done. My troops are concentrated on
> the Gallician frontier and can speedily act . . . Your
> Majesty will see, I hope, my desire to fulfill my
> obligations towards her . . . She will always find a
> faithful ally in me.[5]

Thus far Alexander had only helped morally with words; when, however,
a second Austrian army under Archduke Ferdinand invaded the Duchy of Warsaw,
his attitude stiffened and, with Napoleon insisting on the casus foederis,
he issued an order on May 15 for Golitzin's forces to advance into Galicia.
In the meantime the Austrian army had defeated a Polish army under Poniatovski;
had occupied Warsaw, and was advancing along the Vistula towards Danzig. On
Napoleon's advice[6] Poniatovski followed the Vistula upstream (in the opposite
direction of the Austrians), invaded Galicia, and raised a rebellion among the
peoples of Austrian Poland, forcing the Austrian garrisons to surrender. On
May 23 he occupied Lemberg and began organizing a Polsih government appealing
to all Poles to united in the task of liberating their country. Thus a strange
situation developed: the Russian army entering Galicia was facing not the
Austrians but the Poles ! While these events were taking place in Poland, Napoleon
suffered a defeat at Essling on May 21. News of this defeat was received with
joy in the salons of St.Petersburg, but with restraint by Alexander[7] who told
Caulaincourt that he regretted as much the situation of the defeated French
army under Marshal Lannes as if it had been one of his own Marshals.[8]

Napoleon viewed Alexander's expressions of sympathy and encouragement
in a different light" "Compliments and phrases are not armies; it is armies
which the circumstances demand."[9] On June 3, fifty-three days after the
beginning of hostilities, three Russian divisions crossed into Galicia. Archduke
Ferdinand was forced to halt his northern advance, to evacuate Warsaw, and to
retrace his steps back upstream towards the endangered province. The Russian
army's move was belated. Just before the Russian forces had crossed the border,
Napoleon had dictated a letter to Champagny for Caulaincourt in which he
expressed his deep disappointment with his Russian ally:

> The Emperor's heart is wounded; this is the reason why
> he does not write to Emperor Alexander; he cannot show
> to him a confidence he no longer feels. He says northing,

he does not complain; he keeps to himself the displeasure he feels, but he no longer appreciates the
Russian alliance . . . Forty-thousand men which Russia
could have sent to the Grand Duchy would have rendered
a veritable service, they would have at least kept up
some illusion of a phantom alliance.[10]

Two days later Napoleon expressed his views concerning Russia to

General Savary, stating that "this is no alliance I have there. They have all

given a rendez-vous to themselves on my tomb, but they dare not meet."[11]

At this time an odd situation was developing in Poland: the Russians

and Austrians, officially at war with each other, were both facing the same

enemy, the Poles, who were the official allies of the Russians. Poniatovski

urgently called for Russian help to stop the Austrian columns which were

advancing in the direction of Sandomir; Golitsin, however, moved so slowly

that he came too late to prevent Sandomir from falling into Austrian hands. At

the meeting between the Russian and the Polish commander it was agreed that

Poniatovski should cross to the left bank of the Vistula while Golitsin would

remain on the right bank.[12] At the same time an emissary of the Archduke Ferdi-

nand, Major Fiquelmont, was received at the Russian Headquarters where he

received Golitsin's assurance that the Russians would not go beyond the Vistula

to the west, or, in the south, cross the line stretching from the river Visloka

(a confluent of the Vistula) to Sanok, along the river San to the Carpathian

Mountains. Thus a definite secret agreement was reached between the Russians and

the Austrians on June 22 by which the Russian forces stopped at the agreed

demarcation line, freeing thus the Austrians to re-occupy Lemberg.[13]

Napoleon was enraged when he heard of the slow Russian advance and how,

because of it, Sandomir had fallen. He dictated a letter to Champagny in which

he expressed his displeasure:

Can the junction of the Russians with the Polish army
be marked only with a reversal and by the loss of a
conquest which the Poles knew how to make and guard by
themselves ?

Napoleon carefully avoided any accusation against Alexander and

consequently added:

This no doubt is not the intention of Emperor Alexander,
but he should know with what manner his intentions are
fulfilled; this will help him to put himself in a position in which he commands will have to be obeyed.[14]

Poniatovski, operating separately, occupied Cracow on July 14 which
had been evacuated by the Austrians. In the city, however, he found Russian
Hussars barring his way. The Russians, realizing the importance Cracow had for
the Poles (it was, besides everything else, the holy city where the Polish
kings were buried) also occupied the city, creating thus an impasse which could
easily have errupted into open warfare had the commanders of both armies not
agreed at the last moment to divide the city into two zones and occupy it
jointly. This Russian move plainly showed that the Polish question was a major
issue between France and Russia about which the Czar was not willing to compromise. "I want to be reassured at all costs,"[15] Alexander demanded, subordinating
any future cooperation with France to the question of the re-establishment of
Poland. Rumiantsev handed a note to Caulaincourt on July 26 in which the Russian
fears of a re-established Poland are expressed and demanding an explanation as
well as an assurance against a re-establishment of Poland.[16] The Russian government had not specified the guarantees it demanded, but even if it did, Caulaincourt was no longer authorized to give any.

Napoleon's war with Austria was nearing the end. After their initial
success at Essling, the Austrian armies fought with varied success until their
defeat at Wagram (July 6) after which their resistance crumbled.

On May 6 Napoleon had a letter written to Caulaincourt forbidding him
to sign anything concerning the future of the House of Austria, or to enter into
any kind of negotiations.[17] On July 12 an armistice was signed at Znaim between
France and Austria which was followed by the Peace of Vienna, signed on October
14, 1809.

In the Russian note of July 26 Alexander reminded Napoleon of Russia's
participation in the war, apart from expressing himself frankly about the Polish
question. On the other hand, this note indicated that Russia was not going to
participate in the peace negotiations placing thus the responsibility of the
maintainance of the alliance squarely upon Napoleon's shoulders. Alexander also
wished to avoid antagonizing Austria for Russian participation in the peace
negotiations, accompanied by direct demands for Austrian territory, would have
resulted in Austrian hostility.

In the peace treaty of Vienna, Austria lost, apart from the territory
which Napoleon added to Illyria, the province of Galicia. The future of this

this province rested entirely in Napoleon's hands. Rumiantsev's note of July 26 commented upon the seriousness of the Galician problem, without, however, suggesting a solution. Napoleon's comment to Champagny concerning it was, "You see as well as I do, there is always an uncertainty in what that Cabinet wants; it seems to me that they could have expressed themselves better about an arrangement for Galicia."[18]

In deciding the future of Galicia, Napoleon abandoned the idea of making it a separate state and annexed it to the Duchy of Warsaw, with the exception of the district of Tarnopol, a small section of Eastern Galicia, which he allotted to Russia. To the Duchy of Warsaw the addition of Galicia meant an increase of 1,336,983 souls to its population. The district of Tarnopol which went to Russia consisted of 400,000 souls. A small region, including the town of Brody, remained under Austra.

In a letter to Alexander on October 14 Napoleon explained his decision and pledged himself not to aid the renascence of Poland, adding:

> The prosperity and well-being of the Duchy of Warsaw demand that it be in Your Majesty's good graces, and the subjects of Your Majesty can take it for certain that in no case, in no hypotheses, they can expect any kind of protection from me.[19]

The Franco-Austrian war proved the weakness of the Franco-Russian alliance; the half-hearted advance and assistance of the Russian army and the whole-hearted enthusiastic help by the Polish army must have convinced Napoleon as to the value of one or the other partner in this war. The Peace of Vienna was hardly signed, when Napoleon raised another issue which was to put the alliance to a further severe test.

The Austrian Marriage

The problem had first appeared in the form of a rumor during the Erfurt Convention.[20] Now that the Peace of Vienna was concluded and Napoleon had decided to seek a divorce from Josephine, Caulaincourt was instructed to discuss the matter frankly with the Czar.

On November 22 (eight days before asking Josephine for a divorce) Napoleon asked Caulaincourt to present an official request to Alexander for the hand of Anna Pavlova, the Czar's sixteen-year-old sister.

The decision, however, about any marriage of any of the Czar's sisters was not up to Alexander. According to the will of Emperor Paul, the Dowager Empress, Maria Fedorovna, was to have the final word in the question of the marriage of her daughters. Caulaincourt had previously warned Napoleon that "the first ostensible step was to approach the mother."[21]

Napoleon was too proud to allow such a decision to be made by a woman, especially by one who referred to him as "that atheist." Consequently, on November 22, he dictated a letter to Champagny for Caulaincourt in which he instructed his ambassador to speak to Alexander as follows:

> I have reason to believe that the Emperor, urged by the whole of France, is disposed for divorce. Can I ask if one can count on your sister ? Think it over, Your Majesty, for two days and give me your frank answer, not like to an ambassador of France, but to a person concerned for both families.[22]

This letter, however, was never sent. Just when it was ready for dispatch, Napoleon was informed that Russia was demanding written assurances against the re-establishment of Poland. These Napoleon was not willing to give.

Instead, Napoleon decided to sidetrack the issue. To begin with, he ordered important festivities to be held in Paris on December 3rd, 4th and 5th, during which he showered Kurakin with signs of great respect and friendship. On the 4th he spoke to the Corps Legislatif in Paris during whoch he said:

> My ally and friend, the Emperor of Russia, has reunited to his vast empire Finland, Moldavia, Walachia, and a district of Galicia. I am not jealous of anything good that can happen to this empire, my sentiments for its illustrious sovereign are in accord with my policy.[23]

It was with words that Napoleon attempted to placate Alexander and to bring him into a mood in which the proposed marriage could be arranged. On December 12, Champagny forwarded Napoleon's speech to Caulaincourt with an added commentary by Napoleon for the latter in which Caulaincourt should, when given the opportunity, confront Rumiantsev with these words:

> You must note that there is nothing in the past
> that the Emperor did not do; in the Austrian affair
> you were colorless. How did the Emperor act ? He
> gave you a province which pays more than the expenses
> you had in this war, and he declared aloud that you
> have re-united Finland, Moldavia and Wallachia to
> your Empire.[24]

Caulaincourt's further orders were to stress the following three
points:

(1)   That the Emperor prefers the sister of the Czar of Russia.

(2)   That one counts here the moments, as everything is a political
        affair; the Emperor is in a hurry to assure his great interests
        with children.

(3)   That one should not attach any kind of importance to conditions, not
        even that of religion.[25]

Nothing was heard in reply to this proposal until February 5,1810,

when two dispatches arrived from St.Petersburg in Paris, dated January 15

and 21. In these dispatches Caulaincourt cited Alexander's words concerning

his difficulties with his mother who raised numerous objections. The excuses

Maria Fedorovna used were, first, the tender age of her daughter; later she

objected to her daughter's marriage to a "divorced prince;" still later she

demanded time as marriage was not "a thing to be decided in a hurry." Etc.[26]

It is doubtful whether Alexander at all considered Napoleon as a future brother-

in-law; otherwise and most asuredly, he could have used his influence and power

as Czar with his mother. As matters stood, Alexander was content to hid behind

his mother and plead for time.

The evasive answers indicated to Napoleon that a final decision would

not be forthcoming from St.Petersburg, or, if it did, it would be negative.

Hence, on February 6,1810, Count Schwarzenberg, the new Austrian ambassador, was

approached with a marriage proposal for Marie Louise, the eighteen-years-old

daughter of the Austrian king (emperor). Schwarzenberg forwarded Napoleon's

proposal to Vienna from where Metternich (who originally hinted to Napoleon that

Austria would react favorably to a proposal for the Archduchess) sent the

following reply on February 14:

> . . . Our last dispatches will have shown you that our
> august master, having only the well-being of his people
> in view, would not refuse to give the Archduchess to
> the Emperor of the French.[27]

Metternich considered Napoleon's proposal a way to end Austria's miseries, though knowing that it would not necessarily mean the abandonment of Napoleon's further plans. In a letter to Schwarzenberg on February 19, he expressed his views as follows:

> . . . We are far from deceiving ourselves as to the very great distance there is between the marriage with an Austrian Princess and the abandonment by the Emperor Napoleon of the system of conquests; but we do not despair of turning to profit the moments of repose which necessarily would begin for us, in order to consolidate our internal affairs and temper the views of the Emperor of the French.[28]

Having received a favorable answer, all that remained to be done for Napoleon was a way to inform Russia of his decision without provoking any displeasure from Alexander.

When Napoleon had decided to approach Austria he convened an extraordinary Council consisting of the King of Holland, the Viceroy of Italy, Cardinal Fech, great dignitaries, ministers, and the presidents of the Senate and the Legislative Assembly, to discuss with them the method to adopt pertaining to Russia. The Council unanimously favored an Austr an marriage, the question of religion being one of the main motives. The idea of installing a foreign priest at the Tuileries was considered "shocking" and would "imply an inferiority which would offend the nation." Even if this were possible, "the Emperor's companion and Empress of France would have neither the religion of her husband, nor that of any of her subjects."[29]

With these opinions in view, Napoleon sent a letter to Caulaincourt on February 6 in which the latter was to explain to the Czar that -

> . . . even people who do not hold much for religion cannot get used to the idea not to see the Empress participating in the church ceremonies at the side of the Emperor; that the presence of an orthodox priest (pope) presents an even greater inconvenience . . . that sometimes girls remain two years between the first signs of nubility and maturity and that, therefore, the Emperor does not intend to remain three years without a hope to have children.[30]

The very next day Napoleon worked on a schedule for the arrival of Marie Louise in Paris; taking into account the length of time it would take for his courier to arrive in Vienna as well as Mar e Louise's participation

in the carnival of her native city. The date for the Archduchess's arrival
was set for March 26.[31]

Marie Louise went through three marriage ceremonies. On March 11,
1810, she was formally married to her absentee husband, who was represented
by Marshal Berthier, in Vienna. Then she moved with 83 coaches and carriages
for fifteen days to reach Compiègne on March 27. Marie Louise and Napoleon
were united by a civil ceremony at St.-Cloud on April 1, and, the next day,
by a religious marriage in the Louvre. During all the ceremonies and feasts
it became obvious that Russia had to give way to Austria. Concerning this
fact Metternich wrote to Francis Joseph on April 4:

> The position of your Majesty's ambassador at Paris is
> now the same as that of the Russian ambassador before
> the last war. Everyone pays him attention, and the
> French public, always following the impulses given by
> the court, give them a coloring on the present occasion
> which did not exist formerly.[32]

The Russians seem to have been aware of the possible implications
of the Austrian marriage. Already when the first news arrived at St.Peters-
burg they were disagreably surprised. "This marriage produced a strange
revolution here," wrote Caulaincourt to Talleyrand, "everybody throws stones
at the Dowager mother."[33]

As for the Czar himself, he showed no anger when he heard about
Napoleon's change of plans and the impending marriage with Marie Louise. "He
was too proud to show his annoyance," and he wanted that his felicitations
arrive in Paris before any other." For this purpose he chose the Prince
Alexis Kurakin (the brother of his ambassador in Paris) as envoy extraordinary.[34]
Champagny tried hard to convince Rumiantsev that Napoleon's marriage with an
Austrian princess did not mean in any way that the Emperor was "marrying
Austria with the Archduchess," but that France's policy remained unchanged -

> The Emperor holds to the Emperor Alexander by sentiment,
> principle and conviction of the happy effect this alliance
> has for Europe, and His Majesty wanted me to let you know
> under these circumstances his particular intentions and
> wishes: they have but one aim, it is to be always a friend
> and ally of the Emperor Alexander.[35]

Yet, it would be hard to assume that the effect on the relations
between France and Russia was not profound, all the more so since, at the
very same time, the negotiations concerning Poland had reached a new impasse.

N O T E S

1. Rumiantsev to Alexander (January 30,1809) in A.Vandal, Napoleon et Alexandre Ier, Vol.II, p.52.

2. Metternich to Stadion (February 9,1809) in Metternich, Memoirs, Vol.II, No.135, p.325.

3. Metternich to Stadion (February 17,1809) in Metternich, Op.cit.,No.136, p.326.

4. (C)orrespondance de (N)apoleon Ier, XVIII, 14843.

5. Letter published in the Revue de la France moderne, June 1,1809, quoted in A.Vandal, Op.cit., p.72.

6. Instructions to the Chief of Staff, March 30,1809, in C.N.,XVIII, 14975.

7. A.Vandal, Op.cit., pp.92-3.

8. Caulaincourt's report (June 14,1809) in A.Vandal, Op.cit.,p.93.

9. Champagny to Caulaincourt (June 2,1809) in A.Vandal, Op.cit., p.94.

10. Quoted in A.Vandal, Op.cit., p.95.

11. Memoires du Duc de Rovigo, IV,145, quoted in A.Vandal, Op.cit., p.96.

12. A.Lobanov-Rostovski, Russia and Europe 1789-1825, p.186.

13. F.v.Demelitsch, Metternich und seine auswaertige Politik, Vol.I.,pp.20-21.

14. Champagny to Caulaincourt (July 10,1809) in A.Vandal, Op.cit., p.104.

15. Caulaincourt's report (August 3,1809) in A.Vandal, Op.cit., p.113.

16. Ibid.

17. C.N., XVIII, 15164.

18. Quoted in A.Vandal, Op.cit., pp.120-1.

19. C.N., XIX, 15926.

20. Cp. p.22.

21. National Archives (February 4,1809) quoted in A.Vandal, Op.cit., p.181.

22. Bignon, Histoire de France depuis le dix-huit brumaire, IX, pp.64-5, quoted in A.Vandal, Op.cit., 182-3.

23. Moniteur, December 14,1809, published in C.N., XX, 16031.

24. C.N., XX, 16035

25. Champagny to Caulaincourt (December 12,1809) in A.Vandal, Op.cit.,p.193.

26. Caulaincourt to Champagny, in A.Vandal, Op.cit., pp.254-5.

27. Metternich to Schwarzenberg, in Metternich, Op.cit., No.154, p.379.

28. Metternich to Schwarzenberg, in Metternich, Op.cit., No.154, p.379.

29. Champagny to Caulaincourt (February 8,1810) in A.Vandal, Op.cit., pp.262-3.

30. C.N., XX, 16210.

31. Instructions to Champagny in C.N., XX, 16218.

32. Metternich, Op.cit., No.157, p.393.

33. Quoted in A.Vandal, Op.cit., p.298.

34. Caulaincourt to Champagny (March 17,1810) in A.Vandal, Op.cit., p.291.

35. Archives of foreign affairs (not dated) quoted in A.Vandal, Op.cit.,pp.285-6.

PRUSSIA 1807-1812

Although the Prussian issue did not play a part in the rupture
between Napoleon and Alexander, it was nevertheless an important factor as
both Emperors were interested in this State for different purposes. Alexander
insisted that Prussia should be maintained, even though weakened and deprived
of several provinces. Napoleon regarded it as a French conquest where and from
where the French army could operate as need demanded it, though he would sometimes also refer to Prussia as an "intermediary power" or "barrier" between
France and Russia.[1]

The new Prussian State after the Peace Treaty of Tilsit was reduced
by 2,851 square miles and deprived of 5,158,000 souls, remaining with 2,856
square miles and a population of 4,598,000 souls.[2] "Out of deference to His
Majesty the Emperor of All the Russias," Napoleon consented to list the names
of the Prussian territories he was pledging himself to evacuate (Prussia, Pomera-
nia, Silesia, and Brandenburg) in Articles IV-VIII and X-XII of the Tilsit
Peace Treaty;[3] the evacuation of Prussia by French troops was further confirmed
by the separate treaty signed between France and Prussia at Koenigsberg on July
12, but the evacuation was made dependent on and subject to the fulfilment of
the payment of contributions of 154 million Francs, as stipulated in Article IV.[4]

The enormous financial demand made on Prussia postponed indefinitely
the French evacuation as Prussia was unable to raise this amount. This provided
a diplomatic victory for Napoleon inasmuch as Russia had no right to interfere.
Champagny stated it very plainly in his letter to Savary on November 8,1807.[5]

A partial evacuation of Prussia, however, did take place when, in July
and August 1808, French forces suffered several defeats in Spain and when Napoleon
was forced to send his Grande Armée from Germany to the Peninsula.

The Erfurt meeting which in September 1808 served the purpose in view of
new complications - the Spanish and Austrian threat to the Napoleonic Empire -
to reaffirm the alliance between the two Emperors[6] was not directly concerned
with Prussia. But Napoleon's continued presence in or hold on Prussia was an
essential part of his control of the Continent and indirectly - at least by way
of securing the connection with or access to Poland - contributed to the increasin
friction between the two Emperors.

The evacuation of Prussia by French forces did not entail any
reduction of the financial demands; on August 11,1808, a draft was presented
to Prince William, the brother of King Frederick William, and the Prussian
ambassador in Paris, von Brockhausen, which clearly showed Napoleon's intentions concerning Prussia - apart from not redicing the financial demands, he
attempted in three ways to secure his military control of the country: the
fortresses on the Oder, Stettin, Kuestrin, and Glogau were to remain occupied
by French troops; at the same time Prussia was to reduce her own forces to
42,000 men; finally, in a case of war with Austria, Prussia was to put at
France's disposal an auxiliary corps of 8,000 and later 16,000 men.

Napoleon was motivated by two considerations. One of them was based
upon strategy, as revealed in his reply to a Russian demand for the evacuation
of Prussian territories. Napoleon countered the demand with the argument that
he needed Prussia as a flank against Austria, adding that as long as Russia did
not evacuate the Danubian Principalities he would not evacuate the few troops
he left in Prussia.[7] Moreover, Napoelon was enraged against Prussia on account
of two intercepted letters which had fallen into his hands and which had been
written by the Prussian minister Baron von Stein. In these letters Stein wrote,
inter alia, that the resentmnet was growing daily in Germany and "it is advisable
to nourish it further and to influence the people."[8] There was a strong anti-
French party in Prussia and, besides this, ministers such as Stein and Scharnhorst tried to persuade Frederick William to side with Austria against France,
as "this battle will decide the fate of Europe as well as of us."[9] Frederick
William was against such a step. On August 23 Scharnhorst wrote to Stein: "The
king shows a serious distrust in his people and Austria, but he trusts Russia.
One must oppose his prejudices by showing him Russia's and the Czar's weakness
at all times."[10] But the king was unwilling to accept such advise.

At Erfurt, Prussia's plenipotentiary, Goltz, approached Alexander
to obtain a better deal for Prussia, but the Czar confessed that Napoleon
was too enraged about the anti-French intrigues by Stein and that a modification
of the French demands could only be sought for after the original stipulations
had been ratified. Consequently, on September 8,1808, Prussia ratified the
demands Napoleon had made on August 11.

On his return journey to Russia Alexander visited Frederick
William at Koenigsberg (October 20-24,1808) whom he informed that his
efforts on behalf of Prussia with Napoleon had been in vain and that Stein
should be dismissed "as a political necessity."[11] Stein, considered by
Napoleon a public enemy, eventually fled to Austria.

The Erfurt Convention made Napoleon master of the lands around
the Vistula through the French occupation of Danzig, Thorn, Modlin, and
Warsaw; the Oder was securely in French hands through their occupation of
Stettin, Kuestrin, and Glogau; the line of the Elbe was also under direct
French threat through the French garrisons at Hamburg and Magdeburg,, while
their ally, Saxony, held Wittenberg, Torgau, and Dresden. Thus, while
Prussia's army, according to the stipulations of September 8, did not exceed
42,000 men, Napoleon possessed between the Rhine and the Elbe 70,000 men in
addition to 70,000 to 80,000 troops of Poles, Saxons, and Westphalians.[12]

Prussia, thus kep within Napoleon's military pincers, was reluctant
to take any independent political action as long as Russia showed no signs
of willingness to support her. It is thus no surprise that the news of the
Franco-Russian agreement at Erfurt was received in the Prussian capital "like
a thunderbolt."[13]

Through the crisis of the Austrian War, the Prussian government took
an ambiguous attitude towards Napoleon. Without being encouraged by Russia,
Prussia attempted to form closer links with the anti-Napoleonic forces. Secret
negotiations noth in Vienna and London, however, resulted in no tangibel
results. Stadion, the leading Austrian minister, declared that a treaty was
not necessary as Austria's war was a war for both Austria's and Prussia's re-
establishment anyhow and that Austria, fighting for its very existence, would
never sign a peace without Prussia.[14] The negotiations with England, for the
landing of English troops in the region of the lower Elbe, were a failure too.

On May 12 Frederick William asked the Czar's promise not to become
Prussia's enemy if he should join Austria in her war against France, and, on
May 18, he wrote to the Austrian Emperor that he would jojn the war when his
army was ready. The Czar answered on May 19 with a statement that he would
remain faithful to his obligations to Napoleon, adding that Austria could not
save Prussia but would cause her own downfall.[16]

In the meanwhile Austria had started the war and one of her armies under the Archduke Ferdinand was advancing northwards along the Vistula, entered Warsaw by the end of April and reached Thorn by May 18. The further progress of this army was to be in the direction of Prussia where Ferdinand hoped to be joined by Gebhard von Bluecher and other Prussian commanders. This plan, however, was thwarted with Russia's entry into the war forcing the retreat of Ferdinand's army.[17] The war turned out badly for Austria, but even after the armistice of Znaym on July 12, both Austria and Prussia still maintained to hope of being able to turn the tide. On July 24 Frederick William again wrote to the Czar warning him that Prussia would be lost if Napoleon forced Austria through a peace treaty to join his system. The king also added the following adminition:

> How different the situation would be if you, Sire, would act in the interest of your empire and would abandon the present system and declared yourself against France . . . It seems to me that if Russia, Austria, and Prussia would be determined to continue with their efforts, supported by England and Spain, they could force Napoleon, even if his luck in war should continue, to make a peace which would guarantee freedom for Germany.[18]

This letter remained unanswered until after the Peace of Vienna on October 14. In his reply Alexander remarked that he expected difficulties from Napoleon because of Prussia's attitude during the past war, but that he would make every effort to smooth them over if the king would support him in his attitude towards France; "only with care, patience, and steadfastness in the accepted system can one hope to reach the goal."[19]

To pacify Napoleon and also to find out the French intentions, Frederick William sent Major Krusemark to Paris to congratulate Napoleon upon concluding the peace. Krusemark was received in audience with Napoleon on November 5 and the latter immediately opened the subject of Prussia's re-armament, telling Krusemark that it would have been sheer madness if Prussia had made war against him with Russia at her back. Napoleon also complained that Prussia did not offer him an auxiliary corps, which he would have considered a "loyal move," and that she had ceased her payments . . . "I demand that Prussia pays me what she owes me. If the necessary money is not available, the king can pay with dominions and land."[20]

On December 13 Napoleon wrote to his Prussian ambassador, Saint
Marsan, with the order to undertake serious steps to receive payments from
Prussia, because "if one had the money to mobilize troops and collect 10 -
12,000 horses, one was also capable of paying."[21] Napoleon wanted to know
further why Frederick William could not reduce his forces to 6,000 men and
thus be able to pay from the money saved - "the military party is out of season
in Prussia," he remarked, adding:

> If the king is unable to pay, let him hand over a province.
> I will set a time-limit. If Prussia has neither done one or
> the other by then, I will send my troops and occupy the
> land again. I know how I shall get paid.[22]

On February 12, 1810, Napoleon sent another letter to Saint Marsan to
demand a Prussian province, without however mentioning Silesia or Glogau, but
to say to Krusemark "that everything is possible except that the Emperor becomes
a toy of a few intriguers."[23] Napoleon was more outspoken to the Princess Thurn
und Taxis, the sister of the Queen of Prussia, to whom, in an interview on
February 27, he sharply said: "If the king is unable to pay let him cede Silesia
to me."[24] It is thus obvious that Prussia's plight was meant to serve his purpose
and to strengthen the connection between France and Poland.

In the desperate situation in which Prussia found herself during the
Spring of 1810, Frederick William recalled the man who already once before tried
to save the country - Hardenberg, exiled by Napoleon from the Prussian capital,
but now allowed to return upon Saint Marsan's recommendation that he could find
the money.[25]

Hardenberg realized that Prussia was situated between the devil and the
deep sea. His policy, consequently, was therefore designed to maintain close
and friendly relations with both Russia and France as well as with Austria, now
close to France through Napoleon's Austrian marriage.[26] To raise the money at
home, Hardenberg established new taxes and revenues and consolidated the debts
of State and provinces into one national debt.[27] In this manner Napoleon could
be satisfied without any cession of territory. Prussia's territorial extent had
therefore remained unchanged when in 1811 the Franco-Russian relations took
a new turn.

Napoleon, antagonized by Alexander's independent stand, especially in the Polish question, decided to act. Without a warning, large French contingents entered Prussian territory in March 1811. They advanced in the direction of Danzig and the fortresses on the Oder. On March 11 Napoleon ordered the German fortresses to be reinforced in great secrecy and Hamburg to be converted into a fortress both against England and Prussia.[28] Everything indicated an approaching crisis and Prussia was forced to decide between France and Russia.

Previously the problem of Prussia involved the military occupation of the country by France. Henceforth, in view of the impending Franco-Russian conflict, her main endeavors were directed towards survival between the two powers.

Frederick William was in favor of an alliance with Russia, a sentiment not shared by Hardenberg. In May 1811 a Defensive-Offensive Alliance was offered by Prussia to Napoleon which was rejected on July 9. A similar alliance was then offered to Russia on July 16 which was also refused on October 15.

Obviously, neither Napoleon nor Alexander desired such an alliance with Prussia because it would have indicated preparations for a war. Both sides were arming and preparing themselves secretly for the struggle to come, maintaining at the same time outward pretence of continued friendly relations. An alliance by one party with Prussia would have precipitated a declaration of war by the other side before all preparations were ready.

Frederick William tried one more time for an alliance before throwing in his fate completely with France. On November 20 he offered an alliance to Austria which, however, also refused to enter into any kind of arrangement and replied to that effect on January 3,1812.

On January 29 Prussia no longer negotiated, "she solicited and implored."[29] Napoleon, in Saint Marsan's words could be certain that the king and his ministers were ready to sign and agree to anything he demanded.

The treaty with France was drawn up on February 24 and ratified on March 5,1812. By this treaty Prussia was forbidden to enlarge her army and the existing forces were put under French command. The entire country, except for Potsdam, was open to the French army and the provisioning of troops was made the responsibility of Prussia.[30]

The was Prussia's capitulation after a five-year struggle for survival and political independence. Napoleon occupied the major part of the country, for, as he wrote to his Commander-in-Chief, the Prince of Neuchatel, on April 23,1812: "The best way of assuring Prussia's tranquility consists of rendering it so powerless that it cannot make one move."[31]

N O T E S

1. Napoleon to Alexander (July 4,1807) in (C)orrespondance de (N)apoleon Ier, Vol.IV, 12849.

2. Massovitz: Kurmark, I,581, quoted in M.Duncker, Aus der Zeit Friedrichs des Grossen und Friedrich Wilhelms, III, p.282.

3. Cp. Chapter I, p.5.

4. G.F.de Martens, Recueil des Principaux Traites de l'Europe, VIII, pp.668-70; see also Chapter I, p.5.

5. This letter is given in Chapter I, p.8

6. Cp.Chapter II.

7. Caulaincourt, Memoires, II, p.272.

8. Letter to Wittgenstein (August 15,1808) in Stein, Briefwechsel, Denkschriften und Aufzeichnungen, II, p.489.

9. Ibid.

10. Ibid., p.495.

11. Quoted in M.Duncker, Op.cit., p.296.

12. Napoleon to Davout, August 23,1808 (C.N.,XV,14269); Napoleon to Soult,Septembe 10,1808 (C.N.,XV, 14309).

13. Schladen, Tagebuch, p.345, quoted in M.Duncker, Op.cit., p.304 (April 1809).

14. Quoted in M.Duncker, Op.cit., pp.304-5.

15. Ibid., p.305.

16. Ibid.

17. Cp.Chapter III, pp.26-29.

18. Quoted in M.Duncker, Op.cit., pp.307-8.

19. Ibid., p.310.

20. Ibid., p.311.

21. C.N., XX, 16046.

22. Ibid., XX, 16046.

23. Ibid., XX, 16242

24. Quoted in L.v.Ranke, Hardenberg, III, p.145.

25. Napoleon to Saint Marsan, in C.N., XX, 16479 (May 16,1810).

26. Cp. Chapter III, p.33.

27. Details are given in L.v.Ranke, Op.cit., pp.169-73.

28. Napoleon to Davout, March 13,1811, in C.N., XXI, 17465.

29. Saint Marsan to Maret, quoted in A.Vandal, Napoleon et Alexandre Ier, III, pp.284-5.

30. Quoted in M.Duncker, Op.cit., p.443.

31. C.N., XXIII, 18661.

THE FRANCO-RUSSIAN DISPUTE OVER POLAND

Napoleon's first direct relations with Poland began in 1806 when, after defeating Prussia at Jena, he came into direct contact with the Polish army and Lithuanian levies which drove the Prussians from the town of Kalicz while the French troops occupied the city of Posen. These events resulted in a closer Franco-Polish cooperation. Napoleon's sympathies were limited by military considerations, while, on the other hand, the Poles hoped for a re-establishment of their partitioned land and saw in a union or alliance with the French a means for such an accomplishment.[1]

Under Napoleon's protection a committee of insurrection was organized in Warsaw to which Napoleon referred in his letter to Davout on November 14,1806:

> ". . . Permission should be given to the richest men of the country to form regiments of Uhlans at their expense, also to those who organize national guards at Posen and in other towns, and that a committee of the most powerful men should be formed to organize military and administrative insurrections. Take only part in these through advice and verbal promises and make it known that I cannot declare myself until I see the Poles organized and armed.[2]

On November 19 Napoleon received a Polish deputation from Posen to whom he declared that,

> France has never recognized the partition of Poland . . . If a grand nation, if several million people want to be independent, they will always succeed in their enterprise; as Emperor of the French he will always see with great interest the resurrection of the Polish throne . . . but it depends more on them than on him if the priests, nobles, and citizens want to make common cause and take the firm resolution to triumph or die . . . That what was overthrown by force can only be re-established by force; what was overthrown because of disunity, can only be re-established by unity.[3]

With such statements Napoleon encouraged the Poles for action. Polish hopes received further encouragement when Napoleon visited Warsaw on January 2, 1807, where he participated in all festivities and where he wooed and won the heart of the eighteen-year old Countess Maria Walewice-Walewska. "Poland will become more dear to me if you have pity on my poor heart," Napoleon wrote the countess.[4] After ignoring the Emperor for a while (for she was a modest and strongly religious young woman), the Countess, encouraged by her seventy-year old husband,

by many prominent Polish noblemen, and by Prince Poniatovski, emulating Esther
of the Old Testament, sacrificed herself upon the altar of patriotism. Soon,
however, the feelings of sacrifice turned into l'amour for the Emperor to whom
she eventually bore a son. This was one of the more glamorous episodes in
Napoleon's career and a truly romantic interlude in a generally dreary warrior's
life. For it, unfortunately, no space can be provided here.

Napoleon's pro-Polish policy in 1807 was directed against Russia, as
is justifiably pointed out by Vandal who stresses that, "what Napoleon always
wanted from the eastern regions was a means of breaking the concert of our
enemies."[5] Napoleon needed the Polish troops who played a prominent part at
the battles of Eylau (February 8) amd Friedland (June 14). This auxiliary Polish
army consisted of 39,000 infantry in addition to various cavalry units, making
a total which surpassed 50,000 men. The commander of this force was Prince Jozef
Antonu Poniatovski.[6]

The relations between Napoleon and the Poles provide the background for
the final regulations concerning Poland in the Franco-Russian Treaty of Peace and
Alliance of Tilsit.[7]

In these treaties the Duchy of Warsaw was established under Article V at
the expense of Prussia and was to be governed by Napoleon's ally, the King of
Saxony, on terms "assuring the liberties and privileges of the peoples of the
Duchy." The city of Danzig and its environs became a Free City. The free navigation
of the Vistula was stipulated in Articles VI and VIII. The Duchy in 1807 covered
some 30,000 square miles and had a population of approximately 2,050,000 souls.

By the Convention of Dresden (July 22,1807) Napoleon reduced almost
to nil the powers of Frederick Augustus, King of Saxony, and now Duke of Warsaw,
who was bound to consult the French Resident at Warsaw. Since Frederick Augustus
spent most of his time at Dresden, the French Resident made all the decisions anyway.
The last word on Polish affairs rested, as can be expected, with Napoleon. This
is clearly indicated in the Emperor's letter to Davout on March 31,1808, when he
urged the maintainance of "the utmost possible harmony with the Russians and
restrain the Poles who are hot-heads."[8]

The mode of administration in the Duchy was completely French. The
Constitution, a genuine Polish creation, though following French example, was that
of May 3,1791, which stipulated that the King of Saxony be entitled by inheritance

to the Polish throne. A French resident minister was appointed in Warsaw to
exercise control over the authorities of the Duchy. The King had tried to
nominate a Viceroy, but in the end did not do so. A Council of Ministers,
nominated by the King and selected from a panel drawn up by the provincial
assemblies (the gentry), acted as advisory body and prepared administrative
enactments and decisions. The King also maintained a contingent of 30,000 Poles
who were under the immediate control of Marshal Davout. Prince Poniatovski, the
minister of war, succeeded in incorporating into this army the so-called Northern
Legion - Polish veterans who fought for Napoleon in the previous war - which
remained in the service of France.

Under the Napoleonic system the possibility of local government was
virtually excluded. The constitution envisaged Prefectural Councils for disputes
in each Prefecture, but as these were appointed by the Minister of the Interior,
their pro-French bias was assured. On May 1,1808, the Code Napoleon was introduced.

In complete contradiction, in view of the French hold over Poland, was
Napoleon's letter to Alexander on July 3,1807, in which he wrote that ". . . the
policy of Emperor Napoleon is that his immediate influence does not extend beyond
the Elbe."[10]

As had been noted,[11] the renewed meeting between Napoleon and Alexander
at Erfurt did not result in the prevention of a Franco-Austrian war. In this war
again Polish forces participated and certainly contributed to Napoleon's victory.
Poland's contribution, in contrast to Russia's half-hearted cooperation, resulted
in the enlargement of Poland at the expense of Austria.[12] The part Russia played
during this war in its operations in Poland clearly indicated that Poland had
become a major issue between France and Russia about which the Czar was not willing
to compromise. "I want to be reasured at all costs," Alexander declared to Caulaincourt on August 3,1809, subordinating any future cooperation with France to the
question of the re-establishment of Poland.[13]

The man who exerted great influence on Alexander's policy towards
Poland was his old friend and confidant, Prince Adam Czartoryski, who had been in
charge of Russia's foreign affairs in 1804 and 1805. A member of one of the great
and leading Polish families, Czartoryski had been educated in Russia and had
become Alexander's best friend before the latter became Czar. In spite of his
Russian upbringing and his life at the Russian court, Czartoryski remained a Polish

patriot who never ceased trying to have Poland restored under Russia's protection. Russia already owned vast Polish territories and Alexander was their master; Czartoryski wanted him to become their Lord, but only after restoring Poland into a distinct kingdom which would be closely tied to Russia. Czartoryski's plans were more than pure speculation; they were based upon the reality of a Russian party not only in Warsaw, but also in other parts of Poland. This pro-Russian party existed since the reign of Catherine II and continued to do so in spite of the cruel treatment to which Poland had been subjected during her reign and after. In fact, during the war of 1809, when Galizin's army crossed into Poland, a group of noblemen approached the Russian general in secrecy and offered him immediate allegiance if Alexander would consent to restore Poland and place the country under his rule [14]

Galizin forwarded the proposal to Alexander on June 4,1809.[15] The Czar rejected it, comparing the relations between the two countries with the relations between England and Ireland. He also expressed his suspicions that all the Poles were really after was the restoration of their lost provinces and, after receiving these back, they would detach themselves completely from Russia.[16]

At that time Alexander was still too much under the influence of the alliance with and the promises from Napoleon, but after Napoleon's division of Galicia his suspicions began to grow and he realized that, sooner or later, Poland would be re-established. However, if this should be the case, would it not be better that it should happen under Russian auspices than under French ?

The alliance with France had initially estranged Alexander from Czartoryski. Now Alexander again drew closer to his old friend. In January 1810, he discussed with him the original ideas the two had planned for Poland under Russian rule.[17] Alexander wanted to prove to the Poles that he was their friend and sincerely desired their well-being., He spoke of giving to Poland a new constitution and a separate existence by attaching the kingdom of Poland to the Russian crown.[18]

Any design or plan, however, could only be realized through or with Polish support. Czartoryski was unable to reasure the Czar that his countrymen would accept with enthusiasm a Poland under Russian rule. Alexander, however, was optimistic, for, in his opinion, "the Poles would follow the devil himself if he would lead them to the restoration of their country."[19] It follows, logically, that they would follow Russia which surely was not worse than the devil. Czartoryski agreed with Alexander but remarked that the greatest difficulty was to obtain the

consent of France. Alexander then suggested a sham war with the Duchy of
Warsaw in which the Polish troops might come over to the Russian side and,
together with them, fight against Napoleon. A possible solution might be to
find an indemnification for the King of Saxony by still further dismebering
Prussia, but here again Czartoryski intervened by saying that Napoleon would
never agree to change the present state of things, as he cared much less
for the good of Poland than for the use of the country as a tool in the event
of his making war upon Russia.[20]

These were the considerations and plans which formed the background
for the negotiations between Alexander and Napoleon concerning Poland. After
having finally settled the question of his marriage, Napoleon still had the
important problem of Poland left. Russia had demanded a guarantee with regard
to Poland in November 1809 - an issue which Napoleon had temporarily sidestepped.[21]

The Russian note was sent in the form of a Convention for ratification
to Napoleon on December 23,1809, and contained eight articles with the following
demands:

Art.1. The Kingdom of Poland will never be re-established.

Art.2. The contracting parties will see to it that the denomination
Poland or Pole will never be applied to any part which previously constituted
this kingdom; it will not be applied to its inhabitants or its troops, and will
disappear forever from all official or public acts of whatever nature.

Art.3. The orders of nobility which belonged to the ancient kingdom
of Poland will be abolished and cannot ever be re-established.

Art.4. Nobody of the ancient Poles who are today subjects of H.M.
the Emperor of All the Russias can be accepted in the future in the service
of H.M. the King of Saxony, as Duke of Warsaw; reciprocally, no subject of
H.M. the King of Saxony, in his quality of Duke of Warsaw, can be accepted
into the service of Russia.

Art.5. It is established, as fixed and unchangeable principle, that
the Duchy of Warsaw cannot, in future, receive and extension in territory which
would be taken from one of the parts which constitute the ancient kingdom of
Poland.

Art.6. No more double-nationality subjects will be recognized between
Russia and the Duchy of Warsaw. Those who belong under this term will be given
twelve months, after the ratification of this act, to choose the sovereignty
they wish to adopt, and a term of three years for the appropriation of their
possessions from the one they have renounced.

Art.7. H.M.the Emperor of the French, King of Italy, engages himself to obtain the agreement of the King of Saxony to the above stipulations and the guarantee of execution.

Art.8. The present convention will be ratified by the contracting parties, and the ratification will be exchanged in St.Petersburg within fifty days or sooner.[22]

Caulaincourt accepted and signed this Russian note and forwarded it to Napoleon who received it on February 6,1810. Napoleon immediately wrote to Champagny to prepare a counterproposal to the Russian demands, feeling that he could never ratify the convention in its present form. His instructions and comments were:

> I cannot approve this convention because it lacks dignity. I cannot say that the Kingdom of Poland will never be re-established, because that would mean if one day the Lithuanians, or other circumstances, would re-establish it, I would be forced to send troops and to oppose them. This is contrary to my dignity. My aim is to pacify Russia and to achieve this it is sufficient to revise the articles in the following terms.

> The Emperor Napoleon engages himself never to give any assistance or help to any power or to any internal uprising which would intend to re-establish the kingdom of Poland.

> Article 2 is completely wrong: it is not up to me "to watch that the names Poland or Pole will not re-appear;" such an engagement would be ridiculous and absurd. Instead, an article thus conceived should be put in its place: "The Emperor Napoleon engages himself never to use any kind of public act in which the names Poland or Pole are used to designate lands or people which were part of the ancient kingdom of Poland."

> I cannot ratify Article 3. It is formulated in a too absolute and hard manner; it shoyld be supplemented by an article which stipulates that "one month after the ratification of this convention, the King of Saxony will not create a nobleman of the Order which belongs to the ancient kingdom of Poland. These Orders will be abolished and the decorations and insignia of these Orders can no longer be worn after the death of the actual title-holder."

> There is no change in Article 4.

> Article 6 can remain; but it should be added that those, who took part in the troubles of one or the other power and who wish to withdraw, will receive licenses and their properties will be returned to them if they present themselves within a year.

> You see that these terms resemble very much the others, but with this new edition I maintain my dignity. The Duke of Vicence should announce to the Russian cabinet that the convention he received and concluded has not been approved. The Russians will certainly

worry and imagine that I have great intentions and they will
show their fury; but the Duke of Vicence will immediately shut
their mouths by announcing that he can produce immediately a
convention completely ratified, and that this convention does
not differ in any essential point from the preceding one. Consequently a letter should be written to M. de Rumiantsev in which
you can tell him that I approve of the clauses of the convention,
but that they have not been stipulated with sufficient delicacy,
and that I am sending one which strives to the same end and
which only differs in its redaction.

The counterproposal was sent off on April 12 to Caulaincourt. In a post-
scriptum Napoleon warned his ambassador that such a convention must remain secret
and that neither party could publish it, adding, "I am angry that in making this
convention one has not stipulated that it should remain secret."[24]

Napoleon had good reasons for such secrecy. He did not want the Poles to
get the impression that he was deserting them in any way as one day he might need
their help against Russia.

Napoleon's counterproposal was not accepted by Alexander. Instead, on
March 17,1810, he sent another counter-project. In it Russia's insistence upon
the non-re-establishment of Poland was stressed in Article 1 which now has been
altered to read:

H.M.the Emperor of the French, wishing to give to his ally and to
Europe a proof of his desire to take away from the enemies of
the continental peace all hope of disturbing it, engaged himself,
as does the Emperor of Russia, that the kingdom of Poland will
never be re-established.[25]

Russia's stubborness was very annoying to Napoleon. On July 1 he sent a
letter to Caulaincourt in which he commented about a demarche which Kurakin had made
Kurakin had been concerned with various rumors that Napoleon intended to re-establish
Poland. These Russian concerns demanded strong language and Napoleon used it in
his letter:

What is Russia pretending ? Does she want war ? Why these perpetual
complaints ? Why these injurious worries ? Had I wanted to re-establish
Poland, I would have said so and would not have withdrawn my troops
from Germany. Does Russia want to prepare me for her desertion ? I will
be at war with her the day she makes peace with England. Does she
not get all the fruits from the alliance ? Finland, this object of
so many wishes, so many battles, which even Catherine II did not dare
to want, is it not in its vast expanse a Russian province today ?
Without an alliance, would Moldavia and Wallachia remain to Russia ?

What has the alliance served me ? Has it stopped the war
against Austria which retarded the affairs in Spain ? I
do not **want** to re-establish Poland. I do not wish to end
my destiny in the sands of its deserts. But I do not
want to dishonor myself ridiculous by speaking in a language
of Divinity. No, I cannot engage myself to arm against
people who have not done anything against me, who have served
me well, who have proved to me a perpetual good will and
absolute adherence. In their interest as well as in that
of Russia, I have exhorted them for peace and submission,
but I will not declare myself their enemy and I will not
tell the French people: your blood must flow in order to
bring Poland under the rule of Russia . . . If the Emperor
is angry because of the language Russia uses he is no less
firm in the alliance; he has always marched straight and
without hesitation. He has no political ties with Austria
whatsoever. The Emperor is, with regard to Russia, what
he always was since the peace of Tilsit.[26]

The above note terminated the negotiations concerning Poland. Kurakin
was only empowered to sign a convention such as Russia had sent and which Napoleon
refused to accept. Thus, in the summer of 1810, the project was abandoned.[27]

By this time Alexander must have realized that he could not expect to
come to an understanding about Poland with Napoleon. He hardly ever mentioned
the country again to Caulaincourt, preferring this question to be broached by
Rumiantsev without, however, supporting his minister in any way.[28] While his
words towards Napoleon were full of sentiment and expressions such as, "I want
peace and I want the alliance,"[29] he nevertheless was sending secret agents
into Poland. If his agents compromised him by too great a zeal, he refused to
recognize them and replaced them with other agents. In Austria, too, Alexander
attempted to bring about a change of Austria's pro-French policy of Metternich
to an alliance with Russia through his intermediary Alopeus.[30]

The secret machinations of the Czar in Poland were intended to sway
certain individuals or families in his favor; in Austria the Czar, through
his ambassador Schuvalof, acted more directly and even went as far as to offer
Austria the province of Wallachia in exchange for the province of Bukovina,
a Polish province situated south-east of Galicia, which had been incorporated
into Austria for the past thirty-six years. With such an additional Polish
acquisition the Czar believed to have a better chance to be listened to by the
Poles when the day would come. He might then persuade them that he was destined
to reconstitute Poland under his sceptre.[31]

On November 15, 1810, Czartoryski resigned his position at the
Russian Court and returned to Vilna, in Russian Poland, a curator at the
city's university. Alexander accepted his resignation, especially since he felt
that Czartoryski could further his plans in his native land. With this in mind
he wrote to him on December 25 asking him in great detail to find the true
sentiment in the Duchy of Warsaw. The Czar asked that his request be kept
absolutely secret . . . "I rely upon your prudence, and I feel certain you
will take care not to mar a work to which your country would owe its regene-
ration." Knowing of the pro-French sentiment of the Poles, Alexander mentioned
further to Czartoryski that

> The support on which the Poles can rely is limited to
> the person of Napoleon who cannot live forever. Should he
> disappear from the scene, the consequences to Poland would
> be disastrous: while if by joining Russia and the other
> Powers which would certainly follow her, the moral strength
> of France should be overthrown, and Europe delivered from
> her yoke.[32]

Alexander terminated his letter with an optimistic estimate of the
Russian forces which could oppose the French: on Russia's side he estimated
230,000 men who might at once be reinforced by 100,000 more, whereas France
could only muster 155,000 men.[33]

To this letter Czartoryski replied on January 18,1811, with the
factual statements that, although the sole wish of the inhabitants of the
Duchy of Warsaw was the restoration of Poland, the difficulty in the execution
of Alexander's plane was to produce such a conviction in the minds of the government and army as well as of the inhabitants of the Duchy. He referred to the
feeling in the Duchy that "the French and the Poles are brothers in arms, and
that while the French are the friends of Poland, the Russians are her bitter
enemies - an idea which has been considerably strengthened by the events of
the late war."[34] Czartoryski further drew the Czar's attention to 20,000 Polish
troops and Spain whom their friends and relatives in Poland would fear to
sacrifice to the vengeance of Napoleon. It was absolutely necessary to make the
Poles an offer so distinctly advantageous to their country as to overcome all
personal considerations. To the army estimates Czartoryski responded with some
doubt - "I have so often seen in Russia 100,000 men on paper represented only

by 65,000 effectives."[35] Czartoryski's replies must have given Alexander
little hope of getting the Poles on his side.

The rapprochement with Austria which Alexander tried to achieve
also failed. Metternich was opposed to the idea, seeing great security and
compensation for Austria from Napoleon.[36]

On the other hand, the tensions between Napoleon and Alexander
now began to enter an acute phase. Alarming news began to circulate in the
Duchy of Warsaw of Russian troop movements around the border. It became
apparent that Russia was taking precautionary measures to defend her frontier,
concentrating troops at Vilna, Grodno, Brzecs, and Bialystock, as was indicated
in various letters from French residents at Warsaw. The French garrison at
Danzig was now reinforced. At the same time Napoleon ordered Champagny to
inform Kurakin that these measures were forced upon France by the Czar who
started re-arming on the border.[37]

On April 1 Alexander wrote to Czartoryski: "I have therefore been
obliged t resign myself for events, and not provoking by any step on my part,
a struggle whose importance and danger I thoroughly appreciate, though I do
not believe I shall be able to avoid it." The Czar made clear the part played
by the Polish problem in the aggravation of the situation - "Our projects
have acquired a publicity which could only be very prejudicial to them, so
much so, that they were talked about at Dresden and in Paris."[38]

By this time Caulaincourt had been recalled. In his place Napoleon
sent Lauriston, "a person who I consider will be agreeable to Your Majesty
and the best to maintain the peace and alliance between us."[39]

On June 5, 1811, Caulaincourt arrived in Paris. In a long interview
with Napoleon he attempted to save the Franco-Russian alliance. He believed
that war could be averted if Napoleon gave up his hold on Poland. Caulaincourt
related how the Czar had discussed with him the position of the French troops
which, since the Treaty of Tilsit, have approached 300 leagues towards the
Russian border - "not in the spirit of maintaining the alliance."[40] The Czar
was obviously referring to the forces under Davout in Poland. Upon Caulaincourt's
advice that he should evacuate Danzig, Napoleon replied: "They think they can
treat me like their king of Poland ! I am not Louis XV; the French people
will never suffer such a humiliation."[41] Later Napoleon added that he did not

wish war, but that he could not forbid the Poles to call him and to wait
for him. When Caulaincourt remarked that the Poles would be better off under
Russia, Napoleon broke off the interview.[42]

On August 15 Napoleon demanded to see the archives of his entire
correspondence with and about Russia and he summoned the Duke of Bassano to
work with him on a memorandum. The war with Russia seemed imminent and the
purpose of this memorandum was to give to the public an explanation for the
inevitability of the forthcoming conflict and for the need for new conscription and expenditure.

After commenting about Tilsit and Erfurt and enumerating his complaints
against Alexander's weak and vaccilating policy, especially during the war of
1809, Napoleon stressed that Russia's policy was directed against the Duchy of
Warsaw. The agrandissement of the Duchy after the war of 1809 had alarmed Russia.
Instead, Russia wanted to incorporate the Duchy into her empire, and this would
result in a total destruction of Poland. Alexander had refused his offer at
Erfurt as compensation for the Duke of Oldenburg,[43] demanding instead a compensation from the Duchy of Warsaw amounting to between five and fivehundred
thousand souls which would have been incorporated into the Czar's empire. If
France had agreed to this it would not have taken long before the entire Duchy
would have been incorporated into Russia. In this manner Russia would have
extended her control to the River Oder and as far as the border of Silesia.

In this connection Napoleon made the following historic remark:

This power /Russia/ which Europe had tried in vain to
contain in the North, and which has already advanced by
so many invasions far beyond its natural limits, would
become a power in the south of Germany; she would enter
then with the rest of Europe into agreements which a sane
policy cannot allow; at the same time she would obtain
such dangerous advantages by her new geographical position
in addition to acquiring by the possession of Finland,
Moldavia, Wallachia, and the Duchy of Warsaw an increase
of seven to eight million of her population; such an
increase of force would destroy all proportion between
her and the other great powers. Thus a revolution is
preparing which will menace all the southern States, as
Europe has never foreseen without terror and which the
coming generation will perhaps see accomplished.[44]

In conclusion of his general observations, Napoleon stated:

> His Majesty has thus decided to sustain the existence
> of the Duchy of Warsaw by arms. The interest of France,
> of Germany, and of Europe demand it; policy commands it,
> at the same time honor demands it particularly from
> His Majesty.[45]

Napoleon's thought concerning the Duchy of Warsaw indicate perhaps
better than any other actions or comments, his true policy: the Duchy of Warsaw
was intended to serve as a European barrier against Russia; once this barrier
was endangered Napoleon made it his duty to go to war on behalf of Europe
and allied with Europe in order to prevent the Russian from advancing west. On
the other hand, as can be clearly perceived from his policy towards Prussia
and/or Austria, the "Europe" he had in mind was a French-dominated Europe and,
in this connection, the Duchy of Warsaw held an all-important position.

Vandal comments that the days of August 15 and 16, 1811, constitute
the decisive dates in the history of the rupture of the Franco-Russian alliance.
On these dates Napoleon rejected all ideas of negotiation. Instead, he decided
to assert his aims by the force of arms.[46]

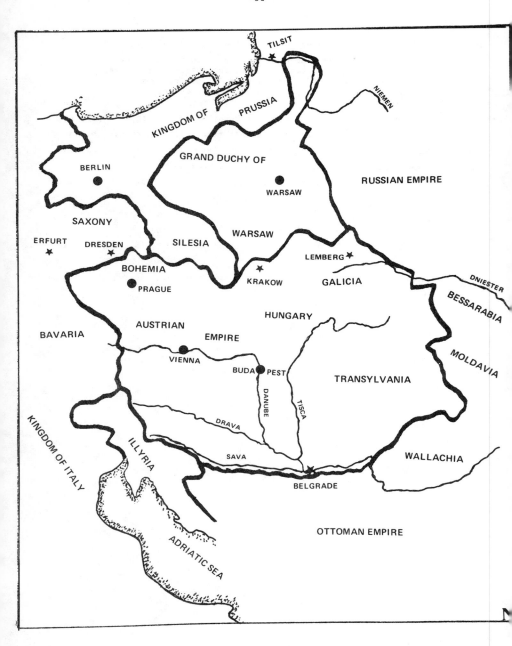

N O T E S

1. Cambridge History of Poland (Chpt.X.A. "Napoleon and Poland" by W.Holland Rose), p.212.

2. (C)orrespondence de (N)apoleon Ier, XIII, Vol. XIII, 11258.

3. Ibid., 11279.

4. Quoted in the Cambridge History of Poland, Chpt.X.A., p.214.

5. A.Vandal, Napoleon et Alexandre Ier, I, p.14.

6. Cambridge History of Poland (Chpt.X.B.,"Military Efforts in Napoleonic Wars").

7. Cp. pp.1-2.

8. C.N., XVI, 13706

9. Cambridge History of Poland (Chpt.XI, "The Duchy of Warsaw,") pp.236-40.

10. C.N., XV, 12849.

11. Cp. pp.19-23.

12. Cp. pp.28-29.

13. Caulaincourt's report quoted in A.Vandal, Op.cit.,II, p.113.

14. A.Vandal, Op.cit., II, pp.329-33.

15. The proposal is printed in full in A.Vandal, Op.cit.,Appendix II, p.546.

16. The reply of June 15,1809 is printed in full in A.Vandal, Op.cit.,Appendix II, pp. 547-8.

17. Czartoryski, Memoirs, II, p.198.

18. Ibid.

19. Ibid., p.202.

20. Ibid., pp.202-3.

21. Cp.pp.28-9.

22. From the Archives of Foreign Affairs printed in C.N., XX, pp.148-9.

23. C.N.,XX, 16178

24. Ibid., 16179

25. From the Archives of Foreign Affairs printed in C.N., XX, pp.153-4.

26. C.N., XX, 16181

27. Footnote in C.N., XX, p.161

28. Caulaincourt's report No.98 (July 18,1810) in A.Vandal, Op.cit.,II,p.428.

29. Ibid., No.101 (August 1810).

30. As accounted a A.Vandal, Op.cit., II, pp.428-9.

31. Ibid.

32. Czartoryski, Op.cit., II, pp.213-18.

33. Ibid., p.217.

34. Ibid., pp.213-18.

35. Ibid., pp.218-22.

36. Metternich, Memoirs, II,. No.178 (March 26,1811), pp.492-5, and No.180 (november 28,1811), pp.499-511.

37. C.N., XXI, 17520 (March 25,1811).

38. Czartoryski, Op.cit., II, pp.228-33.

39. C.N., XXI, 17395

40. Caulaincourt, Op.cit., II, p.286.

41. Ibid., p.287.

42. Ibid., p.298.

43. Oldenburg was incorporated into France on February 18,1811. This act contributed greatly to further Franco-Russian tension. See also C.N.,XXI, 17366.

44. Archives of Foreign Affairs (Russia 153) quoted in A.Vandal, Op.cit.,III, pp.217-25.

45. A.Vandal, Op.cit., III, p.222

46. Ibid., p.226.

THE CONTINENTAL BLOCKADE

The idea of a continental blockade whose purpose was the closing of
the continental markets against England was not Napoleon's original idea. The
concept had been mooted in the councils of the Revolutionary Government at the
time when General Bonaparte was engaged in his first campaigns in Italy. In an
article in the revolutionary organ Redacteur of October 29,1796, the purpose
of such a scheme is expressed as follows:

> Our policy must confine itself to ruining the trade, and
> consequently the power of England by shutting her out of
> the Continent.[1]

On October 31,1796, a law was passed which interdicted the importation
of all English products.[2] The by-product of this prohibition was the stimulation
of French home manufactures.

The leaders of the Republic were convinced of the soundness of such a
policy, and Napoleon, after becoming Emperor, faithfully adhered to it. His
entire policy in connection with other States aimed at furthering this scheme.
After having conquered Austria and Prussia in 1806, he enforced his Blockade Decree
by closing all continental ports against all vessels coming from England or the
English colonies.

The Alliance Treaty with Russia at Tilsit was a severe blow at English
trade as Alexander agreed completely with Napoleon's plans concerning such a
blockade. England's position was best described by Lord Leveson-Gower, when,
commenting about the Franco-Russian Alliance, in July 1807, he said: "The dangers
which threaten England at this moment infinitely exceed what we ever before
apprehended."[3]

England relied heavily for her naval stores (e.g.timber and hemp) upon
Russia. From 1801 to 1805 the trade in naval material had progressed on a larger
scale than ever before and the situation in the Baltic was so favorable to England
that the Navy even considered the construction of warships in Russia.[4] In 1807
a total of 17,000 great masts were sent to England from Riga and St.Petersburg;
this number fell to 4,500 in 1808 and for the following two years to a mere 333.[5]

As for hemp, a good insight into the Russian export of this material
had been provided in a report to the Board of Trade on December 9,1800, by Mr.

Shairp, British Consul for the past 25 years, who stated that:

> ". . . there was no power but Great Britain which had
> any considerable direct trade with Russia - the exportable
> hemp to other countries but Great Britain is very incon-
> siderable. British merchants had such extensive dealings
> in all sorts of Russian articles, as to export from two-
> thirds to three-fourth of the whole of their commodities.[6]

Napoleon and Alexander must have had England's dependence on Baltic
stores in mind at the meeting at Tilsit when they drew up plans for England's
exclusion from this region. Denmark was to ccoperate in this scheme which
provoked drastic countermeasures by England; the British navy's attack on
Copenhagen and the resulting capture of the Danish fleet succeeded in keeping
the Baltic open for the remainder of the Napoleonic wars.[7] Admiral Saumarez
remained in the Baltic from 1808 to 1813 and protected with a powerful fleet
British merchant vessels which managed to draw a certain amount of naval material
from this area even at a time when Napoleon was occupying the shores of the
entire sea coast.[8]

Though the Baltic naval stores, especially those from Russia, were
essential for England, England's general commercial dependency upon Russia
was negligible when compared with Russia's dependency upon England, both from
the point of view of exports as well as imports. In 1804 twelve of the largest
English companies in St.Petersburg controlled half of Russia's exports and a
quarter of her imports. In the Russian coastal cities British citizens comprised
a distinguished colony with their own clubs, estates, parks, etc. The most
important issue, however, was the loaning of capital. British contractors gave
long-term credits to merchants and gentry, which made them largely dependent
upon trading with England.[9] A good insight into this state of affairs was given
by Mr.Shairp in his mentioned report to the Board of Trade when he stated . . .

> the native merchants had grown richer than they used to
> be and they had exprted some hemp on their own account;
> but this was not done without the help and the advances
> from British merchants. The entire trade in hemp depends
> on such advances from British merchants.[10]

Although Russia exported much more to England than what it imported
from there, the imports were, nevertheless, considerable and comprised a
great variety of articles. As far as Russian imports were concerned, a good
analysis of the same was provided by Savary, the French minister, who had been

sent to Russia by Champagny with orders to send back an analysis of the
Russian market.

According to Savary, French trade was non-existent in Russia,
whereas the English trade was in full bloom and comprised "everything in the
world." Thus, from simple items like paper, ink, and pens, to the most
valuable articles, all were in the hands of English merchants, and, as Savary
stated, as long as they remain so the English influence upon the Russian
market will be very strong and, what more, the Russian will become so accustomed
to the English traders that they will regard them as indispensable.[11]

As for the possibility of France taking England's place for imports
into Russia, Savary commented that -

> If we cannot receive special privileges we will not have
> and trade here. Frankly speaking, at present I consider it
> impossible to bring the Russian trade under French influence.
> What is more, I fear that if measures are taken against
> England, the Emperor Alexander will have to take severe
> measures to silence the disatisfied.[12]

As far as Russian exports were concerned, Savary suggested that a
rumor should be started that France, which had not made any considerable
purchases in Russia for a long time, intended to buy timber, linen, and other
commodities from Russia.[13] Such a move would have been important in order to
counteract the effects of the Russian measures against England. In this connection
Savary stated:

> The latests measures which the Russian Government has taken
> against the English have made a strong impression here . . .
> The closing of ports against English ships is regarded here
> as a prohibition against the export of all Russian products
> which England used to buy and export every year in large
> quantities. If this lasts it will be regarded as a catastrophy
> which will affect the interests of the nation . . . One must
> fear that the complaints of the merchants will soon become
> more serious if some forceful measures are not ordered soon.[14]

The French Government attempted to improve conditions and Napoleon had
set aside twenty million Francs for purchases in Russia. Rumors in St.Petersburg
spread that France intended building three warships in Russia. In reality,
however, French trade in the Russian capital remained practically non-existent.[15]

For the first two years of her alliance with France, Russia adhered
strictly to the Continental Blockade. An alien-property custodian had been set up

to direct operations of the sweeping sequestrations ordered by the Czar on
April 1,1808, and May 7,1809, "whereby British property to a large amount and
stores for the use of H.M.Navy and paid for by said British merchants are
now under arrest and the discretion and disposal of the Russian Government."[16]
By 1809, Russian ports were hermetically sealed for English ships.

Due to the lack of English goods, Russian home industries (such as
cloth and silk factories as well as textile mills and distilleries) were developing
throughout the land, but the lack of exports remained a very serious problem
and perpetual ground for complaint from the nobility and merchants which Alexander
could not ignore.[17]

The end of Napoleon's campaign in Spain and his war with Austria marked
an intensification of his Continental Blockade schemes. In 1810 he occupied
territories from the Ebro in Spain to the Waal in Holland; he annexed Holland and
the German coast to the North Sea, parts of Hanover as well as parts of Berg and
Westphalia. His empire stretched as far east as the River Sava in Croatia and the
Dalmatian coast. The more Napoleon was convinced of the eventual success of the
Continental Blockade, the more he realized that he had to come to a definite
understanding with the Czar to secure his cooperation in the measures against
the neutrals as well as to adopt the tariffs which he had introduced as a means
to exclude colonial produce. These tariffs were published in the Decree of Trianon
on August 5, 1810.

The first indication of Napoleon's dissatisfaction with Russia concerning
the Blockade can be found in his letter to Champagny of November 4, 1810, in
which he demanded a strict adherence to the principles of the Blockade. He asked
Champagny to inquire from Kurakin about the colonial merchandise which arrived
at Leipzig from Russia. In fact, Napoleon claimed that over twelve hundred ships,
flying the Swedish, Portugese, Spanish, or American flags, had disembarked
English goods in Russian ports. Napoleon squarely put the blame on Russia, charging
that it depended on Russia if peace would eventuate or war continue.[19] On December
2, 1810, Napoleon addressed another letter to Kurakin through Champagny admonishing
Russia that it should not allow itself to be fooled by false shipping documents;
all merchandise arriving in Europe from the two Indies are brought by English
ships and the Czar, in order to enforce the Blockade, should close his ports
to all ships flying the Spanish, Portugese, Swedish or American flags.[20]

The problem of neutral shipping constitutes a particularly intersting aspect of the Continental Blockade. If the original edicts by both England and France[21] had been enforced at their face value, all commerce in the Baltic would have ceased. Napoleon and his allies could have prevented any ship leaving port, while the British warships could have disposed at will with any ship once it had left a port. As each party, however, wished to maintain its trade while crippling that of the enemy, leakages were inevitable and neutral flags became all-important.

Out of this situation arose the license system of "trading by exception" through maritime indulgences, and both England and France adopted this system which, ultimately, profited England and nullified Napoleon's efforts to crush England's commerce. A good example of this is the city of Danzig where, in 1807, a group of merchants held an audience with Napoleon and "in consequence of a considerable contribution submitted to by this city, English goods and debts will remain untouched." The English representative in this city was Isaac Solly.[22] Napoleon's acceptance of bribes in favor of English trade was emulated by his subordinates. Drusina, the British secret agent who operated under the name of Hahn, reported early in 1809 -

> Notwithstanding the many impediments laid in the way of Trade, several ships have cleared out from these ports (Koenigsberg and Memel) actually bound for Great Britain with cargoes of hemp, flax, linseed, bristles, timber, staves, etc. - The French Consul takes a fee of 1% for himself and a douceur to his secretary for his certificate d'origine. Bonds are also given by the merchants for the return of the ships that do not go to British ports - this is of course pro forma.[23]

The United States, a legitimate neutral, occupied a special position. Prior to 1808 American business ventures to Russia were inconsiderable; in 1810 more than 150 American ships entered Russian ports, sixteen of which spent the winter at Kronstadt, and several at Archangel.[24] Isolated from England under the Tilsit obligation, Alexander expressed the feeling that an American mission to Russia would be welcome. Rumiantsev expressed the same sentiments to Armstrong, the American minister in Paris, explaining that -

> In dissolving our commercial connections with Great Britain, it became necessary to seek some other power in whom we might find a substitute; and on looking around, I could see none but the United States who were at all competent to this object.[25]

In November 1809, John Quincy Adams arrived in Russia as American minister. His problem was to free the confiscated American vessels which had been detained on the suspicion of being English, as, in reality, some vessels had arrived in Russia with false American papers procured in London. Adams successfully accomplished this mission.[26]

In the Fall of 1810 several American ships, passing through the Baltic under the protection of Admiral Saumarez's fleet, docked in Russia. Gaulaincourt tried to throw suspicion on the American cargoes, claiming that one of them, namely sugar, was of English origin. He further raised the question of the certificates of origin.

The _Moniteur_ of July 10,1810, wrote that all clearance and certificates of origin, purporting to be American, were false.

By the end of 1810 relations between Russia and France had considerably cooled off and Alexander was no longer specifically interested to please Napoleon in commercial matters. The arrival of American ships in Russia ports was greatly facilitated by England allowing unopposed passage through the Sound. By the end of 1811 American goods found their way as far as Vienna from where they were sent to Bavaria, Swtzerland, Southern Germany, and even smuggled into France.[27]

Moreover, in the Levant the Treaty of the Dardanelles (January 5,1809) ended the uncertainty of legal trade as far as England was concerned.

On December 31,1810, Napoleon's plan for a Continental Blockade received the heaviest setback. On this date Alexander published his _Ukase_ "concerning the neutral trade for 1811" whicj allowed the import of American merchandise, but prohibited the import of linen, silk, and any other luxury article. In this way he legalized his independent actions by which indirectly he had favored the commercial relations with England and actually had cut loose from Napoleon's Continental System.

To Napoleon's admonition Alexander replied that his feelings had not changed and that he desired the maintainance of the alliance; the _Ukase_ was not directed against French trade, but was for the protection of Russia's trade. Apart from this, it was a purely internal Russian affair about which every government had the right to act alone as long as it did not break any agreements.

By April 1811, Napoleon's mind was made up; as he expressed it to Champagny: "I will make war if this power /Russia/ tears up the Treaty of Tilsit and makes peace with England." [28]

In His Memorandum of August 15,1811, Napoleon further stated:

If France, in order to prevent war, allows Russia to make peace with England, she will never achieve what she has set out to do.[29]

Thus Napoleon realized that Russia's cooperation in the Continental Blockade could only be enforced by war.

N O T E S

1. Quoted in a footnote in A.Fournier, Napoleon I, Vol.II, Ch.XV, p.129.
   Cp.also E.F.Heckscher, The Continental System, p.53.

2. A.Fournier, Op.cit., p.129.

3. Private correspondence of Lord G.Leveson-Gower, II, p.272, quoted in H.
   H.Butterfield, The Peace Tactics of Napoleon 1806-1808, pp.287-8.

4. As accounted in R.G.Albion, Forest and Sea Power, p.328.

5. The total imports into Great Britain of naval stores from Russia and other
   countries from 1799-1815 are given in R.G.Albion, Op.cit.,Appendix D.pp.420-1.

6. Minutes of the Board of Trade Meeting (B.T.5 V 12) quoted in D.Gerhard,
   England und der Aufstieg Russlands, Appendix, p.423.

7. Cp.Chapter I, p.10.

8. As accounted in R.G.Albion, Op.cit., pp.181-2.

9. K.Staehlin, Geschichte Russlands, III, p.133 (for a detailed study see D.
   Gerhard, Op.cit., Ch.II, pp.71-81).

10. Quoted in D.Gerhard, Op.cit., Appendix, p.424.

11. Sbornik, LXXXIII, 266-7 (n.d.) quoted in V.Gitermann, Geschichte Russlands,
    pp.339-40.

12. Sbornik, LXXXIII, 266-7 (n.d.), quoted in V.Gitermann, Op.cit., pp.329-40.

13. Sbornik, LXXXIII, 240-1 (n.d.), quoted in V.Gitermann, Op.cit., p.341.

14. Ibid.

15. Sbornik, LXXXVIII, 438, quoted in K.Staehlin, Op.cit., pp.134-5.

16. R.O., F.O. Russia, 75, quoted in R.G.Albion, Op.cit., p.341.

17. Cp. K.Staehlin, Op.cit., pp.173-4.

18. Details of this Decree are given in G.F.de Martens, Nouveau Recueil de Traités,
    Serie II, I, pp.513-4.

19. (C)orrespondance de (N)apoleon Ier, XXI, 17099

20. C.N., XXI, 17179

Caulaincourt rightly concluded that Constantinople and the Dardanelles
would remain a perpetual stumbling block and, with this in mind, he wrote to
Napoleon on March 16,1808, that if Russia was given the Dardanelles, her
cooperation anywhere and for any purpose would be assured; in fact, any changes
Napoleon desired to make in Europe or Asia, or any guarantees he might demand
from Russia would be accepted by the same without the slightest worry.[9]

Such were the plans which the respective ministers of the two Emperors
worked out, but details of which the two Emperors would discuss and decide at
their forthcoming meeting at Erfurt.

On the eve of the Erfurt Convention, Russia's campaign in Finland was
still in progress. On the other side, Napoleon was preoccupied with his campaign
in Spain. In addition to this campaign bad news had reached Napoleon concerning
the Austrian re-armaments. These two factors created an entirely new problem, the
solution of which became imperative. Consequently the idea for a partition of
Turkey was abandoned by Napoleon, at least for the time being. Napoleon had,
however, to do something about the unfinished negotiations which Caulaincourt
had had with Rumiantsev and the Czar concerning Turkey. Because of the new
situation in Europe, Napoleon called in Talleyrand and entrusted to him the drafting
of a new convention to be proposed to Alexander at Erfurt.

Talleyrand's draft represented the very opposite of the previous schemes.
In it the Principalities were given to Russia, but Constantinople and the Dardanelles were withheld; France and Russia must preserve the Ottoman Empire, except
for Moldavia, Wallachia, and Bulgaria which Talleyrand assigned outright to
Russia. Napoleon added a corrective, pledging Russia for the time being only
to occupy but not to own the Principalities.[10]

The convention Napoleon signed with Alexander at Erfurt shows how
Napoleon had considered and used the Oriental question as a bargaining point.
Now, in order to secure Russia's cooperation in case of a war with Austria,
Napoleon accepted the annexation of the Principalities by Russia (as well as
the annexation of Finland). He also agreed that Russia had the right to negoatiate
directly with Turkey without French mediation. The Erfurt Convention reversed
the policy of a possible partition of Turkey as envisaged at Tilsit. Nothing
more was mentioned by either of the two Emperors about a joint expedition to
India, Asia Minor, Egypt, or Syria. Except for the Principalities, the Erfurt
Convention seemed to indicate Napoleon's renewal to sponsorship of the weakened
Ottoman Empire.

During these protracted negotiations the Russian had been able
to retain their hold on the Danube Principalities. The Slobodzia armistice
had been regarded as too favorable for Turkey by Alexander. He openly
repudiated the same and countermanded the retreat of Russian troops from
the Principalities, ordering them instead to re-occupy the line previously
held. Alexander refused to ratify the armistice and only pledged not to resume
hostilities for the time being. In reality the Russian troops re-entered
Bucharest in the Fall of 1807, several days after the armistice had bee signed.[11]
There they stayed throughout the next year.

In the meantime news had reached the Turks of the Franco-Russian
alliance at Tilsit, provoking deep disappointment and resentment against France.
Sebastiani in his dispatches expressed hilmself very gloomily aboyt Turkey's
future. He expected a renewed war with Russia which the Tuks would begin but
which they would loose. This would mean an enormous expansion of Russia, a
breakdown of Turkey, and anarchy in the Middle East before France could come
to an understanding with Russia about a partition of the Oriental territories.[12]

A new throne revolt which in July 1808 brought Mahmud II to the
Sultanate did not alter the situation. By October 1808 it became evident that
the relations between France and Turkey had reached the parting of ways. Latour-
Maubourg[13] had sent an analysis of France's position in Turkey in which he
mentioned that the Turks "by degrees have lost confidence in us," the greatest
reason for this being the Franco-Russian alliance. The French ambassador further
expressed fear that Frenchmen living in Turkey were exposed to "a certain
danger," adding that Turkish exasperation was quite strong and that Frenchmen
had to suffer insults every day. In any event, he concluded Turkish sentiments
for peace with England had become very strong.[14]

To Turkey Napoleon's vacillating policy was not only disappointing. It
was in the end the cause for a change in their own policy, in the direction
of a rapprochement towards Napoleon's nemesis, England.

****

England had developed an interest in the Dardanelles since the time
she had cooperated with Russia in defending Turkey against Napoleon in Egypt.
In 1806, however, Turkey declared war on Russia on Napoleon's instigation.

This action also upset Anglo-Turkish relations. England reacted by an inten-
sified naval activity which culminated in Sir John Duckworth sailing through
the Dardanelles on January 13,1807, and threatening the Turkish capital.
Eventually, however, Duckworth, fearing that he might get closed-in in the
Sea of Marmara, abandoned the Dardanelles on February 28,1807.

French connivance to Russia's plans gradually turned the balance
again in England's favor and, in summer of 1808, Sir Robert Adair was sent
to Turkey. England's main reason for a rapprochement with Turkey was either
to nullify or at least to weaken the Ottoman decrees favorable to Napoleon's
Continental Blockade and thus re-establish former British trade privileges
with all Ottoman provinces. On November 12, Adair requested permission to sail
through the Dardanelles in the frigate anchored at the entrance of the same.
Britain's good will was further demonstrated with a suspension of all interference with Greek or Turkish shipping.

The impending Anglo-Turkish negotiations were delayed for a time
because of renewed unrest in mid-November. Adair, however, forced the Turks to
a decision by threatening a strict blockade of the Dardanelles and of Smyrna.

In mid-November Adair met with Vahid Effendi and the eventual result
of the meeting was the Anglo-Turkish Treaty of the Dardanelles, signed on
January 5,1809. The agreement restored the privileges of British retail trading
within the Ottoman Empire. The Treaty also contained the following British
pledge:

> As ships of war at all times have been prohibited from
> entering the Canal of Constantinople, viz.the Straits
> of the Dardanelles, and as this ancient regulation of
> the Ottomona Empire is in the future to be observed by
> every power in time of peace, the Court of Great Britain
> promises on its part to conform to this principle.[15]

Secret clauses established a defensive Anglo-Turkish alliance
against France, with England assuming the duty of protecting Turkey with an
adequate fleet. Turkey accepted no reciprocal duty.[16]

****

The Anglo-Russian Treaty brought about a fundamental change in the
relations of both France and Russia with Turkey. Each of the two powers in
counteracting the English took their own independent measures in relation to
Turkey.

News of this successful Anglo-Turkish Treaty ostensibly infuriated
the Czar who threatened the renewal of hostilities of Turkey admitted a British
agent to Constantinople. In reality, however, the news of this Anglo-Turkish
repprochement must have been quite welcome to Alexander. It gave him a pretext
in Spring of 1809 to set his forces in Rumania in movement. In order, however,
not to antagonize Napoleon by this move, Alexander declared to Caulaincourt on
February 11 -

> I do not expect any aggrandizement beyond the Danube. The
> Turks remain where they are. They are necessary there for
> the tranquility of everyone. What we said last year I only
> agreed to in deference to Napoleon and did not intend to
> circumscribe the system we adopted against England.[17]

The war between Russia and Turkey was continued with little enthusiasm
on either side. Upon the end of the Austrian war the Czar moved larger forces
to the Danube. The Russian campaign was marked with certain successes, such as
the capture in 1810 of the Turkish fortresses of Silistria, Sistova, and Rustchuk,
fortresses guarding the passage of the Danube.

On the other side, as far as France was concerned, commercial shipping
in the Dardanelles became a serious issue, especially after April 10,1809, when
the Sultan prohibited all intercourse with Russia "by land or sea" which provoked
a sharp protest by Latour-Maubourg. Throughout the Russo-Turkish armistice the
Dardanelles had been open to French shipping. Now, owing to the renewal of
Russo-Turkish hostilities, Turkey simply proceeded as before and closed the
Straits. The French ambassador's request for permission to be granted to a few
French officers to enter the Black Sea on a small boat was rejected and, upon
Latour-Maubourg's threatening language, Turkey responded that she stood ready
for war if France employed violence.[18]

Further slow progress could only be made when the Franco-Russian
relations began to deteriorate. In February 1811 Napoleon started to act inde-
pendently in Turkey. He re-opened the negotiations for an alliance with Turkey
which had been inerrupted by his alliance with Russia at Tilsit. On February 17
he instructed Latour-Maubourg, through Champagny, to approach the Porte and to
request that a Turkish ambassador be sent to him.[19]

On April 4,1811, Napoleon dismissed Champagny as foreign minister and
also recalled Caulaincourt from Russia. This act of changing ministers who
were in favor of a Franco-Russian alliance, clearly indicated to the world that

Napoleon intended changing his foreign policy. By this time rumors had also
be circulating all over Europe that a French invasion of Russia was imminent.

Almost one year had passed since Napoleon had approached the Porte.
On January 21,1812, Napoleon sent to Latour-Maubourg a draft agreement for a
treaty, secret alliance, and military convention as a basis for negotiations
in Constantinople. The secret treaty promised Turkey the restoration of
Moldavia and Wallachia together with the Crimea in return for which Turkey
was required to enforce the Continental Blockade against England. The military
convention called for Turkey to attack Russia along the Danube if France
attacked Russia through Poland.[20]

This proposed treaty was never signed. Napoleon approach to the Porte
came too late because, by this time, the impending French threat of an invasion
of Russia had definitely altered also Alexander's attitude towards Turkey.

Foreseeing the need for security on his Balkan front, Alexander was
willing to moderate his demands and to begin negotiations with the Turks. The
question of the Russo-Turkish border was the principal stumbling block for an
eventual peace treaty. During the first meeting of the official delegates of
the two powers at Bucharest, on January 12,1812, Russia demanded a frontier
following the river Sereth; the Turks made a counterproposal for a frontier along
the Pruth.

The negotiations lasted several months and remained without results,
mainly due to Russia's insistence on making the river Sereth the border. It
was only due to Rumiantsev's patient policy that Turkey was willing to resume
talks in May. This time Kutuzov for Russia agreed to compromise. On May 17
the preliminaries were signed. Under Article I, the river Pruth from its entry
into Moldavia to its confluence into the Danube was to be the common border
between the two countries. On May 28, the peace treaty between Russia nd Turkey
was signed at Bucharest. Under this treaty Russia received all territories
between the Pruth and the Dniestr which received the name of Bessarabia. Moldavia
and Wallachia were returned to Turkey.

The Turkish question did not directly contribute to the estrangement
between the two Emperors. It rather showed how weak in reality the cooperation
between them really was. In the final phase Alexander had beaten Napoleon to
the draw and the Peace of Bucharest was a serious diplomatic defeat for the

French Emperor. This Russo-Turkish treaty robbed him of his southern flank against Russia in the same manner as he had been robbed of his northern flank (Sweden) by Bernadotte.[21] Thus his great encircling movement against Russia through Turkey and Sweden had failed and he was forced to fight a frontal war without any flanks.

N O T E S

1. Savary's report (November 4,1807) quoted in A.Vandal, Napoleon et Alexandre Ier, I, p.73.

2. Memoirs of the Duke of Rovigo, II, p.79, quoted in V.Puryer, Napoleon and the Dardanelles, Ch.IX, p.180.

3. (C)orrespondence de (N)apoleon Ier, XV, 12886.

4. Napoleon's statement at Tilsit as reported by Rumiantsev in a letter from November 26,1807, in the Archives of St.Petersburg; quoted in A.Vandal, Op. cit., I, p.75.

5. The complete text of this armistice is given in G.F.de Martens, Recueil des Principaux Traités de i'Europe, VIII, pp.689-692.

6. Mentioned in Alexander's instructions to Tolstoi; footnote in A.Vandal, Op. cit., I, p.105.

7. C.N., XVI, pp.498-9 (not numbered).

8. The conversations between Caulaincourt and Rumiantsev,as reported by Caulaincourt to Napoleon (reports 19-25) as well as his letters to the Emperor in connection with his interviews with the Czar and Rumiantsev, are quoted in their entirety in A.Vandal, Op.cit., I, pp.285-306.

9. Quoted in A.Vandal, Op.cit., pp.306-7.

10. According to Talleyrand (Memoirs, I, p.309), the Czar was told that the plan for a partition of Turkey was only shelved and that it would be taken up again after the Spanish campaign was concluded. Quoted in V.Puryear, Op.cit., Ch.XV, p.341.

11. V.Puryear, Op.cit., Ch.X, pp.219-20.

12. Sebastiani's dispatches from February 12,15, 26, and March 4 and 5, 1807, quoted in A.Vandal, Op.cit., II, pp.316-17.

13. Latour-Maubourg was French ambassador in Turkey since March 1808 after Sebastiani had been recalled at his own request.

14. Archives of the French Foreign Ministry; quoted in V.Puryear, Op.cit.,Ch.XV, pp. 347-8.

15. Noradoughian, Recueil, II, No.27, pp.81-5; quoted in V.Puryear, Op.cit, Ch. XVI, pp.362-3.

16. Ibid.

17. National Archives; quoted in V.Puryear, Op.cit., Ch.XVI, p.365.

18. As accounted in V.Puryear, Op.cit., Ch.XVI, pp.370-1.

19. C.N., XXI, 17365.

20. Archives of the French Foreign Ministry (Turkey 222); quote in V.Puryear, Op.cit., Ch.XVIII, p.399.

21. See A.Vandal, Op.cit., III, pp.240-251.

CONCLUSIONS AND OBSERVATIONS

From the foregoing chapters certain conclusions, however tentative, can be arrived at concerning the different factors or reasons which, in a greater or lesser measure, contributed to the eventual break in the Franco-Russian alliance.

The vast scheme of the Tilsit alliance contained in itself the germs for its eventual destruction. With Russia as an ally, Napoleon had envisaged a Europe completely isolated from England and, England thus shut out from the Continent, would be forced to sue for peace. All in all, the Franco-Russian alliance was Napoleon's plan for a Europe dominated by France.

For his partner Alexander, Napoleon promised compensations in the Near East. For the Czar this promise was a re-awakening of an old dream dating back to the Empress Catherine II involving the Straits and the Near East. Yet, having made such a promise, Napoleon's actions showed that his offers were neither serious nor genuine. It was only after the outbreak of the Spanish insurrection and after he had heard of the Austrian re-armaments that Napoleon was forced to make concessions to the Czar in order to secure his cooperation in case of a war with Austria.

The Austrian war showed that Alexander too did not take his commitments very seriously. His half-hearted cooperation with the French forces and his actions at the same time in the Danubian Principalities clearly indicated that he preferred independent action rather than full cooperation with his ally.

The weak support Napoleon received from Alexander inspired him to reward the Poles - Poland received the greater part of Galicia which left but a small token part for Russia. This action could be considered the coup-de-grace to the Franco-Russian alliance. From then on the alliance was nothing but a pretense, a game, which both Emperors used vis-a-vis Europe while at the same time both of them proceeded with their own preparations - Napoleon for an attack, Alexander for defense.

The Prussian issue was a question of principle which illustrated the different ideas both Emperors had as far as Europe was concerned. On the one hand, Alexander wanted to preserve Prussia as an independent state within the European system of states; for Napoleon, on the other hand, Prussia represented the gateway to Poland and, as such, he made it secure by military occupation in order that his lines of communications to Poland be safeguarded.

As far as Poland was concerned, Napoleon had shown that his interest in this revived State was based on the concept that this State should play the role of a European barrier against Russia. Napoleon refreed to it as such in his Memorandum of August 15,1812. In his scheme for a Europe dominated by France, the Duchy of Warsaw held the key position.

Against England, his eternal enemy, Napoleon forced Europe into a trade barrier which would keep England out of Europe by way of the Continental Blockade. For such a plan the support of Russia was essential and Russia, during the first years after Tilsit, cooperated fully in keeping English ships out of Russian ports. The economic results from this Blockade, however, were so detrimental for Russia that Alexander found himself obliged to resume trade with England. The Ukase of 1811 destroyed the purpose of the Blockade and Napoleon realized that only by conquering Russia could he ensure the same.

What about Russia ? How did the Treaty of Tilsit affect its status ?

For Russia the Treaty of Tilsit was not without advantages. At peace with France and her western border secure, Russia proceeded with three wars from which she emerged victorious as well as enriched in territories.

From the Russo-Persian War (1804-1813), which ended with the Treaty of Gulistan, Russia obtained Georgia and a number of other territories.

From the war against Turkey (1804-1812), which ended with the Treaty of Bucharest, Russia obtained Bessarabia and a strip of land on the eastern coast of the Black Sea. This treaty also granted Russia extensive rights in the Danubian Principalities of Moldavia and Wallachia.

By the Peace of Frederickshamn which terminated the war with Sweden (1808-1809), Finland became an autonomous Grand Duchy with the Russian Emperor as Grand Duke.

Added to these conquests and acquisitions must be the gradual expansion of Russia in North America which began in Alaska in the late 18th century. A number of new forts were constructed stretching from Alaska to northern California, where Ft.Ross was erected in 1812.

In the final analysis the Tilsit treaties were of greater advantage to Russia than to Napoleon. Russia emerged as the only major power in Europe other

than France and, undoubtedly, as the most influential power in much of the
Balkans. The breathing space allowed to Russia between 1807 and 1812 made
a number of successful wars she fought possible.

Napoleon emerged from the 1807-1812 period as the "biter bit." He
got something from the Tilsit treaties, but not everything he was after. The
greatest advantage he received was peace with Russia which enabled him to conduct
his campaigns in Spain and against Austria.

An interesting comparison can be made between the Treaty of Tilsit
in 1807 and the Hitler-Stalin pact of 1939. Both parties agreed not to interfere
in the affairs of each other on the respective sides of a line which stretched
from the Baltic to the Aegean. The similarities between 1807 and 1939 are
many and striking and provide an interesting basis for further research.

BIBLIOGRAPHY

PRIMARY SOURCES

Caulaincourt,Marquis Armand de. Memoires, Vol.I, Paris,1933.

Correspondence de Napoleon Ier, Vols.XIII-XXIII, Paris, 1867.

Czartoryski, Prince Adam. Memoirs and His Correspondence with
    Alexander I, ed.by A.Gielgud, London,1888.

Martens, Geo.Fred de. Recueil des Principaux Traites de l'Europe,
    Vol.III, Ser. II,I, Gottingue, 1817.

Metternich, Prince. Memoirs, Vol.II, New York, 1880.

Stein, Freiherr von. Briefwechsel, Denkschriften und Aufzeichnungen,
    Vol.II, Berlin, 1936.

Talleyrand-Perogord,Charles M.de. Memoirs, 5 Vols.,Boston, 1895. Vol.I.

Vandal, Albert. Napoleon et Alexandre Ier, Vols.I-III, Paris, 1891
(contains ambassadors' reports and instructions from foreign ministers).

SECONDARY SOURCES

Albion, Robert G. Forests and Sea Power, Cambridge, Mass., 1926.

Bailleu, Paul. "Die Verhandlungen in Tilsit: Briefwechsel König Friedrich
Wilhelm's III und der Königin Luise," in Deutsche Rundschau, Vol.CX,
pp.29-46; 161-199, Berlin, 1902.

Butterfield, H. The Peace Tactics of Napoleon,1806-1808, Cambridge,1929.

Cambridge History of Poland, Vol.II, 1941 (ed.by W.F.Reddaway, J.H.
    Pensow, O.Halecki, and R.Dyboski).

Clauder, Anna C. American Commerce as affected by the Wars of the
    French Revolution and Napoleon,1793-1812, Philadelphia,1932.

Costigan, G. Sir Robert Wilson; A Soldier of Fortune, Univ.of Wisconsin
    Press, 1932.

Dard, Emile. Napoleon and Talleyrand, London, 1937.

Demelitsch, Fedor von. Metternich und seine Auswaertige Politik, Vol.I,
    Stuttgart, 1898.

Duncker, Max. Aus der Zeit Friedrichs des Grossen und Friedrich
    Wilhelms III, Leipzig, 1876.

Fournier, Karl. Napoleon, Vols. I & II, London, 1911.

Gerhard, Dietrich. England und der Aufstieg Russlands, Munich, 1933.

Gitermann, Valentin. Geschichte Russlands, Vol.II, Hamburg, 1949.

Heckscher Eli, F. The Continental System, Oxford, 1929.

Lobanov-Rostovsky, Andrei. Russia and Europe,1789-1825, Durham, 1947.

Puryear, Vernon. Napoleon and the Dardanelles, Univ.of California, 1951

Ranke, Leopold von. Hardenberg, Vol.III, Leipzig, 1881.

Staehlin, Karl. Geschichte Russlands, Vol.III, Berlin, 1935.

WORKS NOT CITED BUT RECOMMENDED

    Bourienne, Louis A. Memoirs of Napoleon Bonaparte, 4 vols.,New York,1890.

    Cronin, Vincent. Napoleon Bonaparte, New York, 1972.

    Christopher, Herold J. (Ed.). The Mind of Napoleon, New York, 1956.

    Durant, Will and Ariel. The Age of Napoleon, New York, 1975.

    Hutt, Maurice. Napoleon, Englewood Cliffs, N.J., 1972.

    Las Cases, Comte E.de. Memoirs of the Emperor Napoleon, 4 vols.,
                New York, 1883.

    Mossiker, Frances. Napoleon and Josephine, New York, 1964.

    Palmer, Allan. Metternich, London, 1972.